R.E.I. Editions

All of our ebooks can be read on the following devices:
- Computer
- eReaders
- iOS
- android
- Blackberries
- windows
- Tablet
- Cellular

Daphne & Chloé

Californian Flowers

ISBN: 978-2-37297-4844

Published: January 2023

Daphne & Chloé

Californian Flowers

R.E.I. Editions

Book Index

Californian Flowers 11

   Aloe Vera 13

   Alpine Lyli 14

   Angelica 15

   Algel's Trumpet 16

   Arnica 17

   Baby Blue Eyes 18

   Basil 19

   Black Cohosh 20

   Black Eyes Susan 21

   Blackberries 22

   Bleeding Hearth 23

   Borage 24

   Buttercup 25

   Marigold 26

   California Pitcher Plant 27

   California Poppy 28

   California Wild Roses 29

   Call Lilly 30

   Dudleya Canyon 31

   Cayenne 32

   Chamomile 33

Chaparral 34

Chrysanthemum 35

Corn...36

Cosmos 37

Dandelion 38

Deerbrush 39

Dill 40

Dogwood 41

Easter Lily 42

Echinacea...43

Evening Primerose 44

Fairy Lanterns 45

Fawn Lily 46

Filaree...47

Forget Me Not..48

Fuchsia 49

Garlic..50

Golden Ear Drops.......................................51

Golden Yarrow 52

Goldenrod...53

Hibiscus...54

Hound's Tongue 55

Indian Paintbrush 56

Indian pink..57

Iris 58

Lady's Slipper 59

Larkspur 60

Lavender 61

Lotus.. 62

Love Lies Bleeding 63

Mallow 65

Manzanita 66

Mariposa Lily 67

Milkweed 68

Morning Glory 69

Mountain Pennyroyal 70

Mountain Pride 71

Mugworth 72

Mullein 73

Nasturtium 74

Nicotian 75

Oregon Grape 76

Penstemon 77

Peppermint... 78

Pink Monkeyflower... 79

Pink Yarrow.. 81

Poison Oak 83

Pomegranate 84

Pretty Face... 85

Purple Monkeyflower....................................... 86

Quaking Grass 87

Queen Anne's Lace 88

Quince 89

Rabbitbrush...90

Red Clover 91

Rosemary 92

Sage 93

Sagebrush 94

Saguaros 95

Saint John's Wort 96

Scarlet Monkeyflower 97

Scotch Broom 98

Self Heal 99

Shasta Daisy 100

Shooting Star 101

Snapdragon 102

Star Thistle..103

Star Tulips 104

Sticky Monkeyflower 105

Sunflower 106

Sweet Peas 107

Tansy 108

Tiger Lily...110

Trillium...111

Trumpet Vine..112

Violet..113

Yarrow..114

Yarrow Special Formula..115

Yellow Star Tulip 116

Yerba Santa 117

Zinnia 119

Californian Flowers

The Californian Flowers extend the Bach Flowers.
Richard Kats and Patricia Kaminski, founders of the FES (Flower Essence Society), along with the work of other researchers have discovered more than 150 flowers since 1979.
They work on more modern and current specific problems which at the time Bach lived were not as preponderant or were not talked about as they are today: anorexia and bulimia, sexual disorders, diseases deriving from environmental pollution.
It is possible to create composite essences by combining Bach and Californian flowers, as well as essences from other flower therapy repertoires from other parts of the world. Richard Katz and Patricia Kaminski are married, professional partners and directors of the Fes (Flower essence society) since 1980, where they have developed an international network assisted by a group of flower therapists, researchers, psychologists, doctors and botanists who help them in the discovery of remedies. They live and work in California in the northern Sierra Nevada, an uncontaminated place where it is possible to find the essences of wild flowers.
Richard's initial education was mathematics and physics.
But the questions he asked about the nature of science and scientific relevance then led him to a more in-depth study of the human being. He majored in psychology at California State University at Sonoma in 1974.
He then continued by expanding his studies and attending different fields of herbal medicine and botany and meditation.
After intensive work with the original repertoire of dr. Bach, Richard continued pioneering, starting in 1978 to develop the North American plant flower remedies that are now recognized and used throughout the world.
He specializes in the botanical studies of the FES for which he made many of the photos of the flowers.
Patricia's love of plants and animals began in childhood, where she grew up on a farm on the prairies of central Nebraska.

At the University of Nebraska, she majored in and created the "Women's Studies Program" and helped establish a counseling center for female students at the school.

She continued to be active in many areas as a teacher, social services and community organizing.

Patricia first discovered the remarkable effectiveness of Bach flowers in children she followed with learning disabilities, suffering from dyslexia. He has studied extensively in the fields of teaching, healing, and herbal medicine.

Patricia is currently a teacher and counselor for the California Flowers, administering the company's education and research programs. In the research and discovery of flower essences Patricia, Richard and the researchers with whom they collaborate have been greatly inspired by the philosophy of Rudolf Steiner. By studying the botany of the plant, the colour, shape, habitat and other characteristics find a correlation with the properties of the essences.

- Californian flowers exist on the market in 10 ml "stock bottles". To prepare a mixture, two drops of each of the essences of the chosen stock bottles are poured into a 30 ml bottle with dropper; two teaspoons of brandy are added (it serves only as a preservative and can be replaced by apple cider vinegar by increasing the dose) and is filled with natural mineral water.

It is advisable not to enter more than 5 or 6 remedies at a time.

The dose, both for adults and for children, consists of four drops to be taken four times a day under the tongue, unless otherwise specified.

Being a completely natural and non-toxic cure, they have no contraindications, do not cause side effects, can be combined without problems with both traditional and homeopathic medicines (of which they are considered complementary) or other flower therapy remedies.

Aloe Vera

Succulent plant with fleshy leaves, toothed and arranged in a tuft, from the center of which the scape rises with the panicle inflorescence composed of many yellow flowers.
For people who have a lot of energy, but tend to abuse it to achieve their goals, until they feel exhausted and parched with exhaustion due to the total exhaustion of energy due to a great dispersion of vital and creative force. They are so caught up in what they do that they forget to live the rest of their lives.
They have great willpower which they apply fully in their work to the detriment of other aspects of life, but they risk collapse or exhaustion from overusing their resources.
Despite being emotional, sensitive people with not indifferent spiritual potential, they suffocate these qualities by channeling all energy into work or, more generally, material realization.

- The essence acts on the nerves and on the heart chakra, promoting integration between spiritual and vital energy, developing awareness of one's spiritual needs, one's physical limits and the need for rest.

Aloe Vera helps the soul and body achieve greater harmony by providing the nourishment that comes from the aqua polarity of life, the flowing properties of renewal and rejuvenation. When the individual learns to balance his strong willpower with the source of feelings that flows from the heart, there is a tremendous outpouring of positive creativity and spirituality.

Alpine Lyli

For women who do not accept their femininity understood as instincts, genitals, sexuality.
They are very spiritual women who consider sex as something dirty due to cultural or religious conditioning.
This can lead to problems with frigidity or gynecological disorders.
- The flower helps to experience a more intense relationship with one's body.
- For men, the remedy can be indicated to resolve the feminine aspects of the self.

In cases of dissociation from the body, when there is frustration and inhibition of sexuality with lack of warmth and participation in relationships.
Bio energetic support for the exchange between upper and lower chakra energies.
Alpine Lily stimulates the integration of the female soul in the woman, promoting circulation and the exchange of energy between the upper and lower energy centers.
- Alpine Lily indicates to the individual that one's power and potential depends on the expression of both the female body and female spirituality as a whole.

Angelica

Angelica, just like an angel, makes you feel protected and guided during changes or moments of transition and therefore instills strength and courage. Gives the awareness of being protected and guided to those who are afraid of being abandoned to their fate.
This feeling of being protected and protected is of the utmost importance for the inner life of the individual, as it gives him great strength and courage to undertake his work of transforming and healing the world.

- Angelica especially encourages the individual to establish a relationship with the spiritual world, transforming the too abstract perception of spiritual energies into a full sensation of the spiritual presence and spiritual beings.

This awareness is particularly developed towards that world of spiritual beings which is immediately on the border with the human world: the world of angels.
Through a lively relationship with the angelic realm, man receives protection and guidance in daily life, in moments of crisis or in the experience of passing away.

- Useful in moments of great danger when one would like to abandon oneself to despair.

It stimulates the body's internal defenses and strengthens the soul and makes it more aware of its abilities and the true cause of problems. Also useful for those who care for the terminally ill and for pregnant women to help protect the child.

Algel's Trumpet

This flower is used to entrust oneself in the great passage of life which is death. It's useful to face this moment in a serene way, without anguish, overcoming desires and attachments that keep us attached to the physical body.
Transform fear of the unknown into an awareness of spiritual life. Also useful for those assisting dying people.
The most difficult moments can be lived with serene awareness as evolutionary opportunities and not as extremely hard and terrifying trials.
A key word to understand Angel's Tmumpet is trust for situations where it no longer makes sense to struggle with death, or for the surrender of the ego, when the individual must submit totally to a process of spiritualization.

- With Angel's Trumpet the individual is able to experience these processes as joyful transitions instead of frightening ordeals.

The individual realizes that death is a form of birth when viewed from the spirit world, and is able to recognize the spirit beings who are waiting in the other world.
This remedy is of great help for hospice work, warfare, natural disasters, and for all occasions when we are called upon to assist loved ones who are leaving the physical world; it is also helpful for therapists who have to guide the individual through processes of profound transformation, of "rebirth".
Angel's Trumpet facilitates the radical opening of the soul, transforming the fear of death into an awareness of the spiritual life.

Arnica

Useful for both recent and past traumas of various kinds.
In particular, for physical traumas whose memory can be fixed in the body and, therefore, hinder full recovery.
It serves to unlock the memory of the trauma, to bring consciousness out of a state of torpor.

- It reconnects the physical body with the subtle bodies and with the higher ego when dissociations have occurred following violent or traumatic events such as an accident, surgery, emotional shock, drug abuse, unconscious fears related to old traumas.

Useful in problems whose cause is not understood.

- After taking Arnica, the emotional experience linked to the trauma can re-emerge, allowing the necessary awareness to resolve the situation.

It can be used as a first aid, short-term remedy for rapid trauma recovery.
For blackouts and recovery from big scares.

Baby Blue Eyes

People who are unsure of themselves and distrustful and unable to believe in the goodness of the world due to negative or insufficiently reassuring and protective relationships with the father figure (even the absence of the father) which lead to being cynical and detached.

If the father is emotionally or physically absent, or if he is threatening (as in the case of an alcoholic and abusive father), then the child is deprived of a basic sense of safety and security and will grow up with the firm belief that the world is an unsafe place to live.

These people tend to isolate themselves and barricade themselves in cynical (hardening the heart one avoids suffering) or defensive attitudes, therefore, they have serious difficulties in establishing emotional relationships or relationships of any other kind and have great difficulty recognizing the good intentions of others. These souls find it difficult to "let their guard down", so they tend to develop a protective armor of defense mechanisms or intellectual cynicism.

They fear innovations, they shy away from any material or spiritual research.

In the most serious cases they even come to deny their own spiritual needs, because they feel they are dangerous.

- The essence helps to recover the original innocence of the individual and the confidence he had as a child.

The individual is helped to recognize the goodness of others and of the world and, therefore, to accept more, to be more positive and to open up in his expressions and actions.

When you feel far from the innocence and trust typical of childhood especially if abused or abandoned by the father: blame mixed with cynicism, cynism that delays the natural progress of the individual's evolution, numbing awareness.

Basil

For those who tend to separate sexuality from spirituality not considering it possible to integrate them, while in reality they are different expressions of the same energy.
This can lead to consequences such as seeking clandestine sexual relations outside the couple because they are considered sinful.
Strong attraction to pornography and illicit forms of sexuality.
The essence helps to experience the person in his entirety (made up of instincts and spirituality) as sacred.

- Useful remedy for people tormented by fixations, sexual obsessions, blocks or for couples who have problems of sexual understanding.

Black Cohosh

For people who always attract violent situations or live harmful lifestyles. There may be addiction issues or plagiarism.
They have suffered negative experiences in the past that have deeply damaged their self-esteem.
The Black Cohosh personality must learn to contend with the shadow parts of the self and others.

- Black Cohosh individuals are gifted with powerful magnetism and charisma, with particularly strong activity in the lower energy centers, and therefore, they naturally attract many people and threatening situations to themselves, which they must learn to deal with.

They often experience quite tangible feelings of threat or fear, due to real-life circumstances.
In the history of these people, generally, there are situations of violence, abuse or dependence in their own lives, or in the lives of those around them.
Such individuals can easily become ensnared in a vicious circle of destructive energy.
They can push their inner life towards negative thoughts, revenge or even morbid thoughts.
These imbalances may be reflected in physical disease, especially in toxicity or congestion in the reproductive organs or metabolism.

- Black Cohosh flower essence gives such individuals the ability to actively face and transform negative, destructive or threatening circumstances.

In this way, these individuals acquire tremendous power, and learn to balance and harness their inner strength and physical abilities.

Black Eyes Susan

For people who have experienced trauma or suffering so great that it has been removed, but which has led to states of depression, anxiety, anguish, which seem to emerge for no apparent reason.

- This flower helps integrate all that has been removed.

It brings light into the inner darkness, promotes the elimination of emotional toxins by developing the courage to develop the dark side of the personality and stimulate awareness and the positive transformation of emotional experience.
Therefore, it is useful in the case of old repressed traumas, emotional amnesias, insomnia and depression without motivation.
Once the individual Black Eyed Susan can address these buried parts of the psyche and direct them into an appropriate therapeutic environment, they will experience a strong awakening of energies.

- Black Eyed Susan brings back light and awareness, helping the individual to integrate and transform unacknowledged parts of the psyche.

Blackberries

The common characteristic of all bramble species is that they develop even in difficult habitats and grow back despite drastic and radical pruning. It therefore represents the ability to fight to live and fully express one's potential.

- People unable to realize their aspirations and desires or to achieve their goals.

They lack the willpower, ability and energy to implement; they feel blocked and immobilized, they have a lot of imagination and high desires, but they are not able to realize them. Generally, they are subjects in which thought is dissociated from will.
They are people who feel frustrated due to the inability to achieve what they would like or who suffer from the inconsistency between their thoughts and their actions.

- They have high ideals, great aspirations, but lack concreteness, and often also lack of will and decision-making ability, therefore, failing to live as they wish, they suffer greatly.

An aid for conception in women who have difficulty.
In children to develop interest and involvement in homework and duties at school and home. It allows thought to flow into action.
In the group: for those who tend to be idealistic or have an excessively philosophical vision, but find it difficult to commit their will to group projects.
When the light manages to reach the limbs, the individual feels greater inner power to act concretely in the world and to translate what is spiritual into a real change in society.

- Blackberry flower essence bestows this radiant and active light on the will of the human soul.

Bleeding Hearth

This is the essence for those who are to learn the spiritual lesson of love and freedom; it is for those who completely invest their feelings in another person and when the latter is no longer present they find themselves flooded with anguish.
Has a tendency to create relationships based on fear, affective possessiveness, or mutual dependence, inability to love unconditionally.
This intense need to bond is often experienced by the partner as an emotional dependence, provoking the need for detachment, since such a dependent relationship is deprived of true freedom and balanced exchange.

- This essence provides the energetic support to accept the end of a relationship or the loss of a loved one.

It favors the opening of the heart chakra thus giving the possibility to let a feeling flow freely and totally, free and unconditionally.
The loved one is no longer experienced as a property that one fears losing and thus one is freed from affective and emotional dependence.
Many of these people can have an egocentric and excessively self-centered character and tend to discriminate a lot about what is their own and what is other people's.

- The essence helps to separate from possessive relationships, gives freedom in love, allows the partner to grow in freedom.

It helps to process and deal with the painful experience of the first love disappointments, giving the ability to learn not to depend emotionally on others.
With Bleeding Heart flower essence the individual learns to fill himself from within with strong spiritual energies, so that the ability to love the other is based on the ability to respect and nurture the ego.

Borage

For affective depressions.
Who has lived a great pain of heart and now feels the oppression in the chest, a weight in the heart due to pains of love. Brings back serenity, good mood and will to live, soothes pain.

- Gives the courage to carry on in difficult situations having self-confidence (once the plant was called Corago, instead of Borago, referring precisely to the courage associated with it).

When our heart becomes too thinking and sad, we get discouraged, we get discouraged; this essence helps to rediscover lightness of heart, to feel liveliness and lightness, filling the person with energy and optimism.
It is also useful in midlife crises when there is a deep, unexpressed angst and awe at what one has failed to achieve.
In mourning, to overcome the pain of feelings that oppress the heart, due to the death or impending death of the loved one.
Dissipates pessimism, melancholy and all depressive states resulting from exhausting affective experiences. Relieves emotional and mental tensions by restoring good mood, hope and the will to live. It also acts as a purifier of toxins produced by negative moods.

- The lesson to be learned is to face the sufferings and misfortunes of life with strength and courage.

Borage flower essence helps the heart to experience this vivacity and lightness, filling the individual with energy, optimism and enthusiasm, revealing itself as an excellent all-purpose balm and tonic to be used in many compounds, when the person needs to lift himself up. and of encouragement.

Buttercup

They are people who, if they don't match the standards that society assumes, become complexed with little self-esteem which is expressed with shyness and insecurity, little security in expressing inner feelings and convictions.

Unawareness of one's abilities, devaluation of oneself, inferiority complexes due to unawareness of one's own worth.

It is important not to judge conventional standards of achievement and success, but rather to recognize and accept one's uniqueness and unrepeatability as an individual.

This insecurity and underestimation causes attitudes to be taken to attract the attention of others and their approval, therefore, one becomes dependent on the judgment of others; or it can happen that one's desires and aspirations are inhibited out of shame, shyness, fear of failure.

- Also useful in case of physical handicaps that are experienced as complex. Buttercup is the flower essence that helps the soul understand and hold its beautiful inner light which becomes a source of healing and peace.
- Buttercup Flower Essence helps the individual realize and sustain their inner light, which becomes a source of healing and peace for all who use it.

Marigold

Tendency to use sharp or stinging words, people who must be honest at all costs.
They are people prone to controversy, quarrelsomeness, generally not friendly and kind and who are unable to listen to others and use harsh language.
- This flower gives warmth and receptivity in the use of the word in dialogue with others.
- Symbolically it represents the possibility of using the inner light to make contacts with others and interpersonal communication skills evolved through the use of intuition, the organ of perception of the soul.

Increases the ability to give and receive love, warmth, moral support through communication, overcoming the fear of expressing oneself and letting go of resistance in interpersonal relationships. To establish a warm and kind and at the same time deep and correct dialogue avoiding misunderstandings and vain arguments.
For therapists who have to find the right words at the right time or for teachers, therefore in all professions where communication must be intensely developed as strength of mind.
Useful for talkative people who don't know how to listen to others. Word is to be used as a true spiritual and creative force.
- This flower helps balance the active and receptive aspect of communication.

Ability to listen to others without interrupting the conversation.
Marigold is also called "Mary's Gold" (Chorus of Mary), as the golden solar radiance of the Word must be born from the female receptive matrix.

California Pitcher Plant

For people who tend to suffocate, despise, deny their instinctual aspect, linked to physical energies, considering it dangerous and negative.

Other people, on the other hand, let themselves be overwhelmed by instinctual impulses and unreasonably dissipate a lot of energy, reducing the material aspect of life to a squalid physicality.

- In both cases, the floral essence helps to harmoniously integrate physical impulses with spiritual values, allowing one to fully experience the dimension proper to the human being which is physical, mental and spiritual at the same time.

This remedy can, therefore, be used as a harmonizer of the energies of one's three planes when one has difficulty integrating the animal drives present in man and there is an inability to exercise one's control over them.

- They are usually anemic, ethereal people.

It is important for the human soul to learn to distinguish, but not extinguish, its relationship to the animal world.

- It is indicated for people who are unable to integrate their animal side, such as instinctual desires with their sense of human individuality.

California Pitcher Plant helps balance the immense energies of astrality with instinctive desire, so that these energies can strengthen physical vitality and nurture human spirituality.

California Poppy

For those who are attracted to the spiritual and etheric world and resort to charismatic guides, drugs or magical rituals, allowing themselves to be dazzled.

In many cases, when the individual first opens up to a larger spiritual vision, they are pulled in the direction of Lucifer's light; this light seems beneficial, but in reality it stuns and dazzles the person, robbing them of their inner power.

- Those in need of California Poppy are fascinated by spirituality or are drawn to psychic experiences outside of the self, rather than engaging in a balanced process of spiritual and moral growth.

They may be attracted to a broad spectrum of dazzling phenomena, including drug use (especially psychedelic drugs), occult rituals, religious cults, or charismatic teachers.

- California Poppy people can also be mesmerized by social glamor and notoriety, easily identify with the lives of mass media stars, and indulge in whims or ephemeral causes.

Because they do not strengthen and develop a solid inner life, they are often susceptible to techniques and influences which open the psychic faculties too quickly, especially before these energies are balanced with the energies of the heart and thought. California Poppy stabilizes the golden light of the heart, promoting greater self-responsibility and peaceful inner growth. In this way the individual finds the very treasure he seeks, the golden solar force of the reawakened human heart.

California Wild Roses

Apathy or resignation towards oneself and the world, inability to catalyze willpower.
The flower gives enthusiasm for life and the desire to be useful and accept life's challenges.
- California Wild Rose is one of the most beautiful and important flower remedies, as it helps the individual to take possession of his body and to take charge of his responsibilities and duties on Earth. It is often said that hate does not know the opposite of love, but only a distortion of it.

The ability to be truly interested and to give oneself to life, to others and to the Earth characterizes the healthy individual who loves.
Many people hold back or hesitate, not wanting to experience the pain or challenge of life on Earth.
They find it difficult to take emotional risks in relationships with others, preferring instead to make themselves anesthetized to pain and suffering.
Such people may also suffer from deep-seated social alienation, as they fail to ignite the inner fire of the heart for compassionate concern and active agency in society.
- California Wild Rose is a very beneficial remedy for all stages of life and can be of particular help in the adolescent and youthful stages when the individual particularly wishes to find his positive ideals and seeks to make himself useful in the world through his vocation or the job.
- California Wild Rose stimulates the forces of love, so that the individual finds enthusiasm for earthly life, social duties and human relationships.

Call Lilly

For those who are confused about their sexual identity.
For those born of a different sex from what their parents wanted.
Desire to belong to the opposite sex.
- The flower makes one accept one's sexual identity.

It is the essence that allows the integration of masculine and feminine energies, dissolves the confusion about sexual orientation, allowing a harmonious development of the personality through the clear and serene expression of sexuality. Furthermore, it is useful for those people who cannot adapt to social conventions relating to sexuality, who experience homosexual tendencies in a conflictual way, or who cannot find a clear identity because they have homosexual and heterosexual tendencies at the same time.
The lack of sexual identity not only affects the body with frustrations and inhibitions, but creates a deep inner torment that can make interpersonal relationships difficult.
- Calla Lily teaches the individual that true masculine and feminine qualities are found united within themselves, rather than externally in physical or biological traits.
- In this way the personality evolves towards a greater balance and a harmonious expression of the soul.
- For teenagers who find it difficult to relate to boys of the same gender.

Dudleya Canyon

People who are too attracted by magic, by mediumistic practices or in the grip of spiritual fanaticism who neglect practical life, excessively sensitive and suggestible, with a strong tendency to enter trance states that easily detach from reality.

The flower helps to appreciate the value of everyday life experiences. When the individual can be content with his inner life, he need not over stimulate himself with psychic experiences.

- Tendency to fanaticism, lack of objectivity and combative personality, with a certain attitude of vanity and self-respect. Isolated inner life. They refrain from showing their feelings. They are hypersensitive. They think that what happens to them is always worse than what happens to others.

Normally irresponsible people in everyday things, essence helps to put everyday problems, big or small, into their true dimension. They must realize the beauty of everyday life by appreciating the simple things.

During meditative practices we allow ourselves to be attracted by particularly emotional experiences that may seem more important than they actually are and we end up losing sight of the authentic spiritual path.

- The flower helps to channel psychic and emotional energy, frees from fantastic exaggerations and self-aggrandizement, develops inner honesty and discernment, thus allowing to positively satisfy spiritual needs.
- Dudleya Canyon guides you towards a more balanced spiritual openness and a more contained emotional attitude.

Cayenne

For those who find themselves in a stagnant situation and are unable to implement change, they are excessively phlegmatic and complacent, avoiding trying new experiences or new stimuli.

- It is an excellent will stimulant, it unlocks stagnant situations and develops the ability to transform.

For individuals who carry out their activity slowly, who feel stagnant and seem to keep losing strength or lack the drive to continue.
Their will has no energy.
They emerge from inertia only thanks to great stimuli.
Recommended for people who tend to be passive and phlegmatic or for those stuck in a situation of evolutionary immobility.

- This blockage, or these resistances may be due to fear of new experiences or lack of determination or will.

Very useful remedy in phases of physiological change (puberty, pregnancy, menopause) or in situations that require a radical reorganization of life (marriage, divorce, death of an important person, new job, transfer).
Cayenne helps to overcome resistance and hesitation, it helps to become more aware of the evolutionary dynamic in which it is inserted, it stimulates to overcome inner resistance and hesitation which slow down or block the transformation process, developing will and determination.

- The lesson this flower teaches is to learn to move forward to the next stage, learn to change your life, now.

Chamomile

The chamomile flower embodies solar potential and represents the ability to draw on lower energies, to open up and to live fully with serenity and harmony.
Those who need this essence are subject to variable moods and ever-unstable emotions.
Their "inner weather" is stormy and "changeable," until they remember that the sun always shines peacefully behind all outer phenomena.
They tend to accumulate psychological tension throughout the day, particularly in the stomach area. They often find it difficult to relieve emotional stress at night and therefore suffer from insomnia.

- Hyperactive individuals who experience sudden and intense mood swings. They unload their daily stress into the outside world in an uncontrolled way. They are agitated, restless, tense and suffer from unidentified fears.

They are moody, irritable and unable to release emotional tensions. For this type of people it is useful in digestive problems, stomach pain, insomnia and anxiety.
They easily feel hurt in their honor or dignity out of proportion to the cause.

- It is also recommended for apparently capricious children, but who upon deeper observation turn out to be hypersensitive to the environment and for those who often complain of stomach and abdominal pain due to excessive emotionality or who suffer from insomnia .

This remedy favors a harmonious emotional life, because it helps to evacuate tensions and anxieties, re-establishing a balanced and profound contact with vital and creative energy.
It restores inner peace and serenity and therefore allows a more objective view of the experiences that are lived.

Chaparral

For people who have been affected by exposure to disturbing experiences, violent situations or for those who have used drugs and tend to remain dissociated.
The flower purifies the unconscious from disturbed dreams and chaotic inner life.

- Chaparral is an important purifier of the psyche and body, indicated when the individual has been exposed too much to violence, or to disturbing images proposed by the mass media.

It is also a very beneficial remedy for drug detoxification, including medicines and psycho pharmaceuticals, since the use of drugs widens the boundaries of the individual but reduces and distorts rational consciousness.
Thus, the Chaparral individual is damaged by psychic and astral debris lodged in the unconscious and which must be cleared away for full recovery to occur.

- Chaparral is a very important remedy for modern civilization, in which the individual is subject, in various ways, to chaotic, violent and degrading images and experiences. It can be used in many situations, but acts above all through the dream life to purify the psyche.

Chrysanthemum

For those who are afraid of dying (even if they are not sick or elderly) and of growing old. They are people who are attached to material things, highly concerned with financial well-being or social success, and want to accumulate possessions that could be useful in case something happens to them. They reject their own and other people's old age and despair at the passage of time.

People who have lost conscious contact with their spiritual side, therefore, are tormented by the fear of losing what constitutes the object of their identification or what they believe to be the purpose of their life.

Inner discomfort often leads to anguish, depression and real existential crises, especially in the second half of life, when the body, which begins to fade, is no longer able to sustain intense activities. The person therefore has the impression of feeling life slipping out of hand and is afraid of losing everything that until then seemed important to them: youth, luck, success, money.

Essence allows one to accept one's own mortality or the painful losses that occur during life.

The spiritual part of the individual is often erased or blocked, even though it tries to manifest its presence through a strong crisis of conscience (for example, during middle age), through a life threatening illness or through death itself.

- The Chrysanthemum flower gives such an individual the opportunity to be in touch with the spiritual ego and to reflect on the ephemeral nature of earthly things in the light of the Higher Self.

Corn

Philippe Deroide says corn is completely dependent on human civilization to survive and thrive; its grains are too locked in place to be dispersed by wind, birds, or other non-human means. If nobody takes care of them, the cobs fall to the ground and produce many grouped plants that suffocate each other for lack of space, until they disappear.
It needs the human hand for harmonious development.
Its signature lies precisely in this, as it provides balance, stability, harmony, cooperation and exchange.

- For those who have concentration problems or are disoriented in situations where they have to make long-term plans, because it promotes emotional detachment and allows problems to be observed more objectively.
- Excellent remedy for people who live in metropolitan environments, too chaotic and overcrowded and cannot find their living spaces.

It helps those who by nature feel the need for a great deal of space around them and are disoriented or uncomfortable in confined, crowded environments.
Useful for older people who find it difficult to adapt to modern living conditions, congestion, chaos and technology and prefer areas in contact with nature.
Intolerance towards one's body felt like a "prison" of the soul, does not tolerate tight clothing or shoes, or does not tolerate people getting too close to them.
They are dreamy, nervous, easily distracted or lack concentration and cannot adapt to the pressure of big cities.

- The essence helps to find one's roots even if there is no contact with the earth, in urban areas, therefore, to find one's spiritual roots.

Cosmos

For communication problems such as slurred and slurred speech or difficulty with words of people overwhelmed with too many ideas.
They are people who suffer from the frustration of not being able to express their opinions clearly and in particular their deep perceptions often become introverted, shy, insecure.
- It can be of help to teachers, actors, journalists, writers and all the people who carry out an activity in which public speaking is required to maintain concentration, express themselves succinctly and incisively while maintaining emotional detachment. For those who are verbally dominated by anxiety and are generally introverted.

Impatient, nervous, slow in thought and hasty in their speech, they give the impression of being confused and disoriented.
The flower integrates thought with the word, giving clarity to ideas, mental and verbal agility and coherence, allows you to speak with fluidity, tranquility and clarity.
- It needs to be taken for a long time.

Useful for animals because it encourages communication between species; in cases where animals of different species are kept together; to train animals or to establish psychic bonds in the relationship with animals.
Suitable for both the animal and the person who takes care of it.
- Cosmos harmonizes thought and speech with the higher functions so that true spirit can radiate from the personality.

Dandelion

For excessive muscle tension and too much physical and emotional strain and fatigue.
They are people who act at all costs by engaging in various activities simultaneously with zeal and enthusiasm, but for this reason they tend to plan life too much, without taking into account the energy possibilities of their body.
They are intense, passionate, impatient, they don't tolerate waiting.
Lack of psychophysical flexibility.

- The flower helps to listen more to the needs of one's body and to dissolve tensions. It gives the ability to use vital energy to fully experience one's talents, following the indication of intuition which allows one to make the right choices at the right time.

They are very tense, stressed, emotionally unstable and often anxious people because they are overloaded with practical commitments and no longer have the time to devote themselves to reflection, rest and silence.
Being accelerated they fail to learn from experience because they don't give themselves time to stop and learn.
Relieves muscular and emotional tensions, promotes internal and external perception through the body.
As tension is released, the individual gains greater inner tranquility and balance, allowing spiritual forces to flow through the body in a dynamic and fluid way.

- The Dandelion flower teaches how to listen more closely to the messages that come from the body and from the emotions.

As this tension is released, the individual gains greater inner tranquility and balance, allowing spiritual forces to flow through the body in a dynamic and fluid way.

Deerbrush

Lack of clarity of intentions and inner sincerity, inability to make the right choices for one's own ful filment. Unconscious feelings that stimulate outward actions.
They are people who are inauthentic and open in their dealings with others, and who lack the purity of their inner motivations and feelings that dissociate themselves from their outer actions.

- It allows you to be honest with yourself and facilitates coherence between action and thought, so that these people can end up being an example for others.
- Useful for those who act without having a clear vision of the goals they intend to pursue.

Sometimes they lose sight of the goal to be achieved, because they are excessively concerned with pleasing the expectations of others or with preventing the disappointments they could receive from others.
Other times, however, due to lack of awareness and sincerity with themselves, they live in a state of profound confusion and therefore are unable to make the right choices for their own fulfilment. For people who keep important secrets out of fear of being vulnerable, to protect themselves or out of shame.
They are people who avoid honest confrontation with themselves and, above all, avoid analyzing the underlying reasons for their own behavior. The essence gives purity and clarity of purpose, a greater awareness of unconscious desires: it makes the unconscious conscious.

- As the individual Deerbrush develops the ability to understand inner virtue, outer actions more echo the inner being.

Thus the individual Deerbrush radiates truth and harmony and heals others with his presence alone.

Dill

When you have a lot of stimuli around you, but you can't process them, like a kind of congestion of the senses.

It is useful for hyperkinetic children who are unable to learn from the many stimuli they have.

Free from mental congestion when sensory overstimulation has been experienced.

Hygiene of the soul requires that these sensory stimuli be assimilated, otherwise psychic indigestion and nervous breakdown occur.

- In times past, those desirous of spiritual growth sought secluded environments and ascetic living conditions which reduced sensory stimuli and freed the soul for higher spiritual work.

Dill Flower Essence helps bring harmony to the psychic life in the context of daily work and modern life.

With the Dill flower, one learns not only to discriminate and clarify sense experience, but more importantly, to allow sense life itself to become a vehicle for enlightenment.

Instead of being dulled and repressed, the senses can be refined and clarified, becoming even more luminous and transparent.

In this way, a new type of clairvoyance and ultra sensoriality is born in the modern individual.

- Dill flower essence helps the individual transform sensory overload into the ability to perceive the world of the senses as a manifestation of spiritual archetypes.

Dogwood

It has the ability to transform rigidity, inner hardness into physical and emotional harmony. Deep trauma due to violence or abuse suffered in childhood which led to hardening, stiffening of the personality and then of the body.
- For people who feel awkward, awkward, uncoordinated and have constant accidents.
- Emotional trauma deeply rooted in the body, emotions are inhibited, unable to express themselves.
- Lack of coordination in movements and ease in attitudes.

It is used when some childhood emotional trauma resides in the body.
In people who are hardened, resentful, or emotionally defending themselves from punishments, violations, experienced in past periods, they lack creativity.
It allows you to show more affection or love by eliminating the harshness.
For people who are very strict, hard on themselves and who carry wounds from the past. They are inflexible and inelastic in their bodies and usually repeat the abuse and destruction treatments they have undergone, especially seeking violent intercourse or showing self-destructive tendencies and an inclination to accidents. Useful for beaten children, even physically, who later use the body as armor and are awkward, inflexible and graceful.
- The essence restores the original innocence, helps to acquire flexibility, spontaneity, grace, gentleness, calmness, relaxation, tranquility and helps to forgive.

For those who feel awkward and ugly, abused or neglected in childhood that detached them from their innate sense of grace and beauty, clumsy, hurt-prone, accident-prone, awkward individuals, recovering sweetness, grace, innocence and openness, for the misfortune-prone and self-destructive.

Easter Lily

People in conflict with their sexuality, who live it in a degraded and dirty way.
It is difficult for them to reconcile spirituality and sexuality; this can lead to abstinence or tend towards perversion and promiscuity.
Very important remedy for women.
- Easter Lily's white lily has always been a symbol of both purity and sexuality and reproduction, it is extremely conflicting for the individual to integrate the sexual life with the spiritual life.

For good reason, many spiritual paths require celibacy as a condition of spiritual development, it is possible, however, for modern people to reconcile these apparent opposites; which will bring forth new and important possibilities.
Easter Lily is an important remedy to help those people who feel great inner tension between sexuality and spirituality. These conflicts can express themselves in one direction or the other, towards a promiscuity which degrades and damages the astral body or towards a bigotry which separates the person from the vital energies of the lower body.
Easter Lily is a particularly important remedy for women and can help with impurities and problems with the sexual and reproductive organs.
- Easter Lily's most fundamental gift is to enable the individual to fully utilize the psychic energy currents associated with the sexual and reproductive organs.

Echinacea

For people who have been hiding and enduring suffering for a long time, but have been harmed by people and/or events.

- They have experienced humiliations, their dignity has been affected to such an extent that their identity is called into question.

Some examples are being hurt, discriminated against because of race, religion, opinions, sexual orientation, physical problems, age, and not being able to defend yourself because you felt threatened.

Useful for rebuilding and renewing lost self-esteem and self-respect, restoring dignity and for those people who fail because they subconsciously think they don't deserve to get better. It represents the ability to live dignity and self-respect, expressing one's spiritual energies with intensity and in the best possible way.

Suitable for weak, disoriented and defenseless personalities in today's often violent society, tending towards anonymity and lacking in positive models that detract from the dignity of the individual and lead to energy imbalances that weaken the immune system.

- The floral essence stimulates and awakens the true inner self.
- It is an essential remedy when the individual has been subjected to the violence of shocking and destructive forces.

Echinacea recovers the true identity of the ego and the essential dignity of the individual, in relationship with the Earth and with mankind.

Evening Primerose

For people who have experienced maternal rejection in the pre-natal period (during pregnancy).
- Inner conflicts caused by abuse or mistreatment suffered in early childhood, they feel rejected, unwanted by others and by their own mother and this leads them to avoid engaging in relationships, to fear of being parents.

Over the years, those who have lived this type of disharmonious experiences develop a profound sense of loneliness and abandonment, have many difficulties in expressing their emotions and in particular are unable to establish deep and demanding emotional relationships since they put up all kinds of barriers to not deepen one's relationships in order to keep them superficial. The fear of not being wanted or accepted by others prevails in them. They usually have conflicting relationships with their parents.
- This essence used in children eliminates deep wounds of rejection and abandonment.

For those women who want to get pregnant, but consciously or unconsciously fear failure, fear of not being up to the parenting task since they have been deceived in an emotional relationship. This inner emptiness may try to be filled with food or sex, but then feel that nothing nourishes or fuels them.
Emotional blocks, inability to establish deep and committed relationships, they are unable to live their sexuality joyfully.
- Evening Primiose literally reborns the individual by providing a matrix of nourishments that were lacking in the very first sensations of incarnation.

Fairy Lanterns

For the eternal child who refuses to grow up or take responsibility (Peter Pan syndrome).
Insecurity, immaturity, emotional dependence.
Inability to accept maturity.
Resistance to body change.

- They are people who experienced situations in childhood and adolescence that did not allow for harmonious development of the personality. An overprotective, authoritarian, or overly demanding family environment.

Children who have not had the opportunity to express themselves freely, to know and verify their abilities and for this reason have become insecure, fragile, in need of constant external reassurances and tending to maintain relationships of dependence in order not to assume responsibility for their own lives. Or parents and relatives who reinforce the personality of an immature child.
Thus they play the role of the eternal child who needs to unconsciously repeat their childhood into adult life, hoping to somehow transform this blocked stage.

- Also useful for babies who are born prematurely or for those who experience regressions when a little brother/sister is born or for those who are slow learners or lag behind in physical or emotional development. Delayed puberty and anorexic tendencies.

Fawn Lily

They are people who live in isolation, are prone to states of meditation, contemplation and prayer, but are too delicate and lack self-protection to face the world.
They are not capable of living their spirituality in the world.

- People in need of Fawn Lily have highly developed energies of spirituality, so much so that it is difficult for them to deal with the stresses and strains of modern society.

Their souls are naturally inclined to states of contemplation, meditation and prayer, it is easier for them to be in these modes of spirituality than to be too much in the world.
However, the individual may become too mature and overdeveloped in his spirituality.
Fawn Lily people need to sow the great talents they have accumulated in order to evolve and progress, otherwise they become too introverted and emotionally cold, lacking the ability to draw strength and vitality from the physical world.

- Fawn Lily stimulates the innate healing and teaching potentials of such individuals, as the soul evolves from its cosmic virgin archetype into world mother, or world server.

Filaree

For people who lack the ability to take the bigger picture of day-to-day events.

They get totally involved in little things of little importance in which they get lost, and which become excessive and disproportionate, often obsessive worries that make them waste an enormous amount of time and psychic energy.

Annoying, obsessive personalities who are generally very judgmental and in constant disagreement with other people's ways of doing or not doing.

- Excessively preoccupied with minor problems of daily life and physical ailments that limit active participation in life.

Their monotonous way of communicating makes them boring and obsessive in stories; they can be hypochondriacs, because they pay attention to everything. The essence helps to broaden the vision in the daily setbacks. When well directed, these people have tremendous inner strength and reserve, which can be of great value.

They can suffer from tics, tremors and rituals of all kinds.

Attachment to the formal aspects of household management, allowing activities such as cleaning the house to become too important, not allowing the individual to participate in social life.

- Filaree helps these individuals make a fundamental shift in perspective, instilling a more cosmic vision, thus helping them to see the issues of everyday life in the right perspective.

Filaree, in particular, frees the too contracted psychic energy, spreading it more and making it more receptive to the influence of the spirit.

Forget Me Not

For the desperate pain, without consolation, due to the loss of the loved one.
- It helps those who have never been able to overcome the initial stage of anguish, the sense of loneliness and abandonment due to the loss, the pain after the death of a loved one.

For parents expecting a child, because it allows you to establish a conscious relationship already from pregnancy with the soul that is about to start a new life.
For people who need to contact their spirituality.
For those who repress deep pain and hold it on an unconscious level.
They are people who generally prefer to isolate themselves.
- It opens the heart to free it from the pain it contains, ability to integrate the past and the present.

This essence guides us to a greater awareness of the depths, beauty and possibilities of lived relationships with the soul.
It gives greater openness and awareness.
To overcome distress for a person and bestow spiritual vision for the dead person.

Fuchsia

For people who remove emotions such as anger, pain, sexuality, out of fear of their intensity or due to educational and cultural conditioning and somatize them.
There is an inability to express feelings. These repressed feelings resurface in the form of hyper-emotionality.
- They are people who cry easily, have a heightened emotionality that hides deep emotional traumas and accuse various psychosomatic symptoms such as migraine and stomach pain.

This false emotionality or suffering acts as a cover for deeper emotions that appear too strong and heavy to integrate with the psyche. They are people who can pathologically sublimate aspects of the personality (external asceticism).
The remedy allows even the most painful and violent emotions to emerge and to be consciously faced, so that the person can express himself in a more authentic way and free himself from torment.
- It produces a catharsis, the release and knowledge of stifled but deeply ingrained emotions that need to be expressed.

It is the flower that connects us with our emotional "shadow".
For sexuality that is sublimated with other psychosomatic emotions.
The Fuchsia individual learns to recognize pain and other deep feelings more immediately, thus giving the life of the soul the possibility of becoming emotionally authentic and vital.

Garlic

People with low vitality, who are easily influenced, who fear the judgment of others have little will and tend to absorb the fears of others.
They are people who normally freeze in front of others, especially in testing situations or when they have to speak in public.
- The flower develops greater vigor, endurance and strength to face situations that cause terror or paralyze in front of others.

The lesson this flower teaches us is to learn to face fear.
Gives courage to overcome fear, apprehension or nervousness by developing strength.
The Garlic flower recovers the wholeness of such individuals, helping them to consolidate and unify the astral body and bring it into a state of greater harmony with the physical and etheric bodies and with the spirit.

Golden Ear Drops

It allows access to painful feelings from childhood or periods of life in which one is helpless and vulnerable that influence the affective life and that have been removed from consciousness, but continue to influence the person unconsciously.
Amnesia is a survival mechanism, but the unconscious residue must ultimately be addressed before it corrodes, like a poison, the current life.
Inability to let off steam through crying.
- It helps to detach from repressed pain and trauma and reconnect with the positive aspects of one's childhood.

The flower restores a positive connection with one's childhood, brings back memories, favors the understanding of painful events of the past and allows them to be integrated harmoniously with current life.
Golden Ear Drops help the individual remember and reclaim this past, so that it becomes a source of strength, wisdom and clear insight.

Golden Yarrow

For extroverted people who are overly influenced by others and the environment.
They must have a defensive attitude to protect themselves from their vulnerability towards others.
Thus they tend to avoid putting themselves in sight or showing themselves and withdraw into isolation.
Useful for artists.

- Golden Yarrow people often find it difficult to cope with their sensibilities and may turn to drugs or other soul-numbing and hardening actions.

Unfortunately, this also distances the individual from their own artistic abilities and sensibilities.
Golden Yarrow helps such people to build a protective shield that at the same time gives access to their innate sensitivity.
In this way, the individual comes to create an ingrained inviolable light and strength within himself, which protect and encourage the delicate and noble expression of the ego.

Goldenrod

Particularly sensitive to group pressure, Goldenrod people are easily influenced both by the group and by family ties, seeking approval, but in the insecurity they behave in an aggressive and antipathetic manner, for example, making their own the dreams and projects of others.
An inability to resist family pressures on life choices, as well as an inability to understand oneself and to put oneself and others in proper perspective, puts on a false social persona.

- Particularly suitable for teenagers because they are in the developmental phase where the personality is structured and consolidated, but also useful for impressionable adults with a weak character who need to be noticed or accepted.

Of an insecure character, they can have antisocial behaviors that aim to create barriers of separation from the world.
- Goldenrod favors the vertical axis of relationship to one's deep self to counterbalance the horizontal social axis which is too broad and disproportionately influencing the personality.

In this way the Goldenrod individual acquires greater inner strength and conviction, learning to fully balance the two poles of the self and the Other.

Hibiscus

The flower gives warmth to the body and soul, especially taking care of sexuality.
- For women who have a negative image of sexuality due to abuse or violence suffered.
- For men who have distorted images of women, to establish a more positive relationship with female sexuality.

When the person fails to live the instinctual and passionate aspect of his being serenely and with spontaneous sweetness, sexual expression is cold, detached or blocked.
This flower gives women awareness, acceptance and authentic expression of their sexuality, in harmony with the deepest and purest feelings of the heart.
When there is a decline in sexual desire after menopause.
- For those women who experience sexuality with little warmth and desire, who avoid intimate relationships and chronically have little predisposition to initiate actions that lead to sexual pleasure.

They cannot make their sex a place of pleasure, experiencing it as an obligation.
The flower helps to learn to enjoy sexuality.

Hound's Tongue

For those who see the world too materialistically and rationally, with a tendency to be cynical.
This can lead to feeling oppressed or depressed due to too earthly or scientific views.
The flower helps to recover the sense of wonder.
Hound's Tongue stimulates and revives the activity of thinking.

- Hound's Tongue restores to the individual a sense of wonder and reverence for life and also helps him to see clearly and accurately the spiritual dimensions of the physical world.

Indian Paintbrush

For those who are unable to physically realize their creative expression, they are unable to sustain the psychophysical commitment that this entails, having low vitality and physical exhaustion.

- Useful for artists to better express their art.

Many individuals do not fulfill their artistic and creative potential, as they are unable to harness spiritual energy in the right way.
This phenomenon is similar to a current of electrical energy that must be properly polarized and brought to earth.

- Indian Paintrush is specific to these levels of imbalance.

It shows the individual how to use the will or lower metabolic energies to polarize spiritual energy so that the physical body reflects a healthy alignment between Earth and Heaven.
It also helps artists in the qualitative expression of their art, especially if it lacks substance or connection with the physical world and natural processes.
More importantly, Indian Paintrush helps the individual learn how to use their creative potential in great harmony with the physical world.

Indian pink

For those who can't keep their cool under pressure.
Physical energies are easily lost due to excessive activity. This flower helps to stay calm and focused even under pressure.
It is useful for managing everyday annoyances.

- People in need of Indian Pink are inclined to do many things at once and live very intensely, but the astral body gets out of control, as it is no longer stabilized by the ego or Spiritual Self.

Such individuals identify too much with the periphery of the circle and with its agitated movements, rather than with the center which, on the other hand, remains fixed and inviolable.
They are very tense and emotionally volatile and appear haggard and drained because their etheric body is damaged by excessive astrality.

- Indian Pink helps these individuals identify with their spiritual center.

Remaining more contained, they learn to direct their activity with the conscious ego and therefore live in a healthier and more harmonious way.

Iris

For those individuals who feel incapable of acting in accordance with their creative inspiration, who experience themselves "limited" or "arid", who feel frustrated due to lack of inspiration or who, despite having inspired ideas, cannot materialize them.
For artists who feel they no longer have the inspiration, the creativity; for people who feel parched, oppressed by mediocrity because they no longer have ideas.

- Wake up inspiration and artistic creativity.
- It amplifies the qualities of the right hemisphere of the brain.
- It elevates the soul to a more fruitful level of consciousness.

This remedy is particularly suitable for reharmonizing the various states of frustration typical of artists, due to lack of inspiration, a sense of non-perfection or that of loneliness and estrangement from the "normal" world. Amplify the power of intuition.

- It's also very useful for bringing a little color and vitality to people who feel suffocated by the dullness of everyday life and work routines. This flower helps to color life, to cultivate beauty within oneself and in the world.

The essence of Iris incites the individual to create and cultivate beauty, within himself and in the world.
Iris is an excellent and universal remedy to initiate and support individual growth with flower therapy and other therapies; as flowers are the colors of the soul of Nature.
Therefore, Iris helps the inner life of the human soul to be in harmony with the Soul of Nature and therefore to become truly alive, vibrant and "iridescent".

Lady's Slipper

For those who tend to use their head too much and are always tense and nervous.
The consequences can be a decline in sexual performance and a nervous breakdown.
Lady's Slipper helps the individual to more fully integrate their spirituality into the body.

- It especially balances the relationship between the crown chakra and the lower energy centers.

Those in need of this remedy are often unable to realize their own inner power and potential, and therefore their day job or career is only a dim reflection of their real possibilities.
Psychic energy, circulating inappropriately in the body, leads to congestion of spiritual energies in the higher chakras.

- Lady's Slipper people are often subject to tiredness and exhaustion, and above all to a reduction in sexual potency.

Lady's Slipper is a tonic for the nervous system; releases those spiritual abilities that reside in the higher energy centers, making them circulate throughout the body.
This redistribution of psychic energy is particularly addressed in the feet; in fact, the ability to follow one's destiny or to "walk" one's path is closely linked to the intuitive powers that reside in the extremities.
Lady's Slipper calms and restores the nervous system, helping the individual regain self-control and spiritual strength.

Larkspur

For those who tend to be too centralizing, to have too much responsibility or to give themselves excessive importance.

- It helps to experience leadership in order to be a leader who knows how to command in harmony with others, who does not abuse his power, but transmits charisma and enthusiasm.

True spiritual leadership requires charisma or an infectious enthusiasm.
When the individual Larkspur burns with a positive identification with their inner ideals, their altruism nurtures and inspires others. This type of command is therefore not an energetic power manipulating others or a forced and oppressive execution of one's responsibilities; it is rather an inner joy that energizes others.

- Larkspur helps those in leadership positions align their feelings with spiritual ideals.

In this way, the individual learns to spread an inspired charismatic energy that motivates and encourages others.

Lavender

Nervousness and hyper stimulation cause tiredness and a sense of emptiness.
They are people who can't pull the plug, they have physical energy that they can't discharge.

- Lavender flower helps those people who excessively absorb spiritual influences.

They tend to be highly aware and mentally active, with a strong attraction to spiritual practices and various forms of meditation. However they often take in much more energy than their body can actually absorb.

- "Tight as a string" is a typical phrase to describe this type of person.

They mostly have head problems, such as migraines, or vision problems and tension in the neck and shoulders. They are very often afflicted with insomnia or other nervous diseases.
Lavander, first of all, works to sedate and calm these people; at a deeper level, it teaches how to moderate and regulate psycho-spiritual energy.
In this way, the Lavander individual learns to use their highly sensitive abilities in balance with the needs of the body.

Lotus

Catalyst for healing processes, opens to spirituality.
It leads to concreteness those who tend too much to abstract themselves.
Balance between spirituality and physicality.
The individual is predisposed to wear a crown of light and, in fact, is endowed with an imperceptible energy center called the crown chakra; this chakra gives the individual a sense of dignity and an awareness of his royal or divine nature.
But the crown can only be worn properly by the person who has acquired true objectivity and inner humility.

* Lotus is a specific remedy for crown chakra imbalances.

It acts as a spiritual or harmonizing elixir, helping the individual to open up to their inner divinity.
However, an individual can overdevelop his spirituality.
If the crown chakra is overdeveloped in relation to the other energy centers, especially the heart, the Lotus flower brings the spiritual forces back in the right direction and in balance.
Lotus especially cures the tendency towards spiritual pride, or the illusion that the ego is "spiritually perfect or superior".
Lotus is an excellent remedy for inciting and harmonizing the higher consciousness and most importantly for integrating spirituality in a balanced way with the other energy centres.

Love Lies Bleeding

It helps to overcome immense pains and great trials when you no longer see the meaning of your life and are resigned.
The flower helps to find life's great answers, it allows the individual to face and transform pain and suffering.
Inability to accept and transcend both one's own and others' pain, understanding its meaning and value for human experience.
This pain is very intense and is expressed in the form of anguish, deep-rooted physical pain or illness.

- The effect is to push the consciousness towards introversion and the person feels deeply depressed.

But the essence does not directly relieve this suffering, but helps the individual's consciousness outward, from isolation to understanding the purpose of this experience.
Deep melancholy caused by excessive personalization of pain, need to understand that one's pain is part of a greater human experience, awakening love and the meaning of compassion and sacrifice.
The most important teaching of Love Lies Bleeding centers on the meaning of compassion and sacrifice.
Understanding this is referred to as "Christ consciousness," that is, the ability to suffer or "bleed" not for ourselves but for all of humanity and for the redemption of the Earth.

- The ability to understand that one's pain is part of the human condition is key to being able to truly feel love and compassion for all living things.

Sideboard

For those who are easily distracted, are careless, find it difficult to concentrate and tend to be distracted.
They are people who start many things, but then leave them half done.
They are people who do not live enough in the present and for this reason they tend to disperse.
It is also useful in the change of season or in very hot periods where, for example after lunch, we tend to lose concentration or be inattentive.
The individual lives too much outside the confines of the ego and not enough in the present; he easily gets lost in what he does and wastes his energy.

- Madia is indicated for this basic imbalance but it can also be helpful for problems related to the seasons, especially in summer, when the heat makes us inattentive and distracted, or for the lack of concentration we are subject to in the early afternoon.

Sideboard brings the individual back to his center of balance, so that the conscience is well alert and focused.
It helps the individual to embody and direct his vast spiritual potential.

Mallow

For those who want to get close to others, but don't do it out of fear and insecurity. This causes him to create barriers that make him unable to build relationships, because he thinks he is not capable of it and does not trust others enough.
This flower helps people learn to believe in feelings and involves them more socially.
Coldness, detachment, block in experiencing affection, fear or insecurity in dealing with people, distrust.
It is an inability to give oneself to others, not having trust in people or not feeling capable of giving warmth.

- This flower helps the individual to learn to believe in the feelings he has buried deep in his heart, encouraging him to become more socially involved.

Sense of abandonment due to difficulty in relating to others - in adolescence when you have problems maintaining friendships, you feel pressured in the group and not at ease in society - favors involvement with others by giving warmth to friendship.
The Mallow flower gently opens these obstructions to the life of feeling, so that the individual can begin to experience the warmth of social connection, which arises from the loving exchange with others. Mallow helps the individual to learn to believe in the feelings he has buried deep in his heart, encouraging him to become more socially involved.

Manzanita

To accept or rediscover a good relationship with your physical body (for example, during pregnancy, puberty, menopause).
Useful for people who have food problems or for women who reject the female form or their own bodies.
Inner sickness manifests itself as a feeling that the body is hideous and corrupt or that it has little intrinsic value compared to the spirit. The body is often extremely objectified, exploited or emptied by strictly spiritual or ascetic regimes.
Such people adopt restrictions or rituals related to food, with a tendency to bulimia or anorexia.
This rigid view often stiffens the body prematurely and can be the cause of many diseases, despite "perfect" health regimens.

- Manzanita helps the individual to sweeten his relationship with matter and direct his spiritual attention to the body.

Thus the individual comes to conceive of the body as a reliquary or as a temple of the spirit.
Manzanita encourages engagement with the physical world, especially with the body, and teaches that matter is dead or inferior only when it is not accepted by the individual's consciousness.

Mariposa Lily

Unconditional maternal love is a fundamental support for the growth of the child.

- When the relationship with the mother is not harmonious, or is insufficient, the child lives in a state of deep emotional frustration, having the sensation of not being loved. This leads to behavioral distortions almost hostility towards women if you are a man, or refusal of motherhood if you are a woman.

If the person is damaged in his first relationship with the feminine, he feels cold and empty inside and deep inside he feels unloved and unwanted. There is therefore a rejection of the feminine (sweetness, artistic creativity, sensitivity, emotion). This flower also helps to overcome the anguish linked to family traumas such as parents' divorce, the death of one of them, abuse, violence.

For estrangement from the mother or from being a mother due to trauma suffered in childhood.

- For conflicts related to the mother-child relationship, both for the mother to establish a good bond with the child (even during pregnancy), and for the child who has had problems with the mother figure or has not received affection which he needed.

For those who tend to eat to fill emotional voids. Feeling of not being loved, need to forgive mistakes made by one's mother, mistreatment and abuse experienced in childhood
The flower gives greater tenderness, sensitivity.
Expands the heart, gives capacity for consolation.

Milkweed

For people who take refuge in addictions when faced with difficulties to escape from self-awareness.
- They fear responsibility, so they numb themselves with drugs, alcohol, overeating, membership in religious sects, clouding their conscience.

This condition can occur from accidents, trauma, or an ego denial, they can be the result of a problematic process in childhood that creates an ego desire to return to the infantile state.
They are people who feel inadequate and unable to personally manage their own lives and take responsibility for their own evolution, they do nothing on their own, they are very dependent, immature, with infantile behaviors that are progressively stereotyping more and more , until it turns into a very organized and hardened armor of character.
This flower increases one's strength, will and independence.
- Milkweed nourishes the individual on a very deep level, giving him the ability to revive that most essential part of the self that has regressed.

When the individual learns to live the healthy function of his ego, he sees his strength and independence grow.

Morning Glory

For those who have a displaced biorhythm (they wake up tired in the morning and would never go to sleep in the evening), lead an unregulated and hyperactive life and can make a lot of use of caffeine and other stimulants to keep up the rhythms. There's also disorder in how he eats, he's hungry more towards the evening hours or even at night.

- Also useful for newborns who mistake day for night as it regulates the biorhythm. The Morning Glory individual must constantly be alert to align his astral body with its physical/etheric components. The astral body (or star) is naturally drawn towards the forces of the night and, if left unbalanced, does not hesitate to devour the etheric body (or life).

A manifestation of this imbalance is evident in individuals who prefer nightlife and have irregular eating and sleeping patterns.

If this damage continues for a long time, it will be increasingly difficult for the individual to incarnate in the body, not only in the morning, but throughout the day.

Unable to use the natural energy of the etheric body, the person will desire to use stimulants such as caffeine and, in extreme cases, cocaine or amphetamines.

When this astrality continues to dominate, the individual shows symptoms of recklessness and probably even destructive and violent tendencies.

- Morning Glory helps the individual gain greater awareness and respect for life and the vital processes of the body. The Morning Glory individual learns to correct his own rhythms in order to be more in tune with the cycles of Nature. With Morning Glory, the individual learns to experience more natural states of energy and, therefore, the gift of life itself.

Mountain Pennyroyal

For those who tend to absorb negative emotions and thoughts.
This flower gives serenity, purifies the mind of negative thoughts, clarifies and positivizes thought.

- Mountain Pennyroyal is particularly indicated for the mental sphere of the individual, which may be devoid of vitality due to psychic congestion resulting from too many negative or chaotic thought forms.

There may also be mediumistic tendencies in these people, so that they unconsciously absorb the negative thoughts of other people or other entities.
When this condition reaches an extreme level, the individual is no longer able to think clearly for himself or make rational decisions.
Possession tendencies may occur, especially if the person is prone to alcohol or other drug use.
In these cases, seemingly conscious actions are performed on the orders of entities other than the real self.

- Mountain Pennyroyal acts as a purgative; it has the powerful ability to purify and expel negative thoughts or harmful entities that have entered the astral body.

Mountain Pennyroyal clarifies the mental body and promotes greater mental vitality, especially positive and clear thinking.

Mountain Pride

Stimulates the courage to face the challenges we face.

- For those who tend to waver and draw back when faced with challenges and are unable to take a stand if they believe in something.

It is an important remedy for those who seek peace at all costs, but in reality do not realize that they are living passively, instead of actively acting to achieve their goals.
The ability to act on one's concept of truth is of enormous importance; especially in the modern world, it is of fundamental urgency that the individual learns to transform feelings of dissatisfaction or disillusionment with the world into positive energy for change.

- Mountain Pride endows the individual with the archetype of the spiritual warrior, the radiance of the positive masculine for both male and female individuals.

Mountain Pride is an especially important remedy for those people who confuse peace with passivity.
Such individuals must learn that affirmative action is an important healing agent, not only for personal strength and soul development, but also for true world peace.

- With Mountain Pride the individual learns to take a stand in the world and for the world, aligning their personal identity with the forces of goodness and truth

Mugworth

For moody people, who often have mood swings, hyper-emotional. The individual is only half alive if he does not experience himself in sleep.
The body vegetates during sleep, but the soul has the ability to awaken into another dimension of life.
- Mugwort fosters the receptive aspect of the psyche, allowing for greater awareness of dreams, so that the ego can gain greater insight into matters of daily life and can benefit from guidance and direction from the spiritual world.

Mugwort especially helps to navigate the flow of psychic life, without getting lost and without feeling overwhelmed.
It helps balance the transitions between day and night consciousness, causing the individual to remain connected in a healthy way with the practical, physical world.
This balance is very important, as when the lunar energies become too predominant or expressed inappropriately, the individual becomes irrational, hysterical or overly emotional.
Mugwort helps direct the psychic life into its rightful sphere, gradually opening the individual to a wider consciousness.

Mullein

It helps to connect to one's moral conscience for a deep awareness, for those who have not yet developed their scale of ethical values.

- Weak, confused and indecisive people who tend not to be honest with themselves or with others.

They lack inner clarity and are unable to be authentically themselves, they easily change their opinion and behavior out of opportunism, sometimes slipping into insincerity, or they do not have enough fortitude to be consistent with their own ideas. Extremely effective for those who lack moral firmness and who resort to dishonesty or deception in conducting everyday affairs.

- It can help a group of people to develop the collective consciousness, clarity of thought, fairness and solidarity necessary for the realization of a common project, despite social pressure or confused social trends.

In pregnancy, when you are in doubt whether or not to keep the baby, it helps to get in touch with your moral values.
For people who are undecided about the direction they want to follow in their lives with respect to their values.
For people who don't have clear moral values, they lie and can't tell the difference between good and bad, for example in psychosis. Helps develop patience and balance enthusiasm. It strengthens the spine, and this has to do with its shape that looks like a standing sword.
It allows us to find the truth in ourselves and face the world.
With Mullein, the individual listens to their inner voice and develops the ability to listen and respond to the inner self.

Nasturtium

For those who work too much with their head and lack physical energy.
Being excessively intellectual has led him to live life aridly without verve and vitality.
It is ideal in the phases of life in which study or career require very active intellectual activity.

- Nasturtium is indicated for times when the individual overuses or overstretches the thought energies so that they are no longer in alignment with the lower, metabolic energies of life and heat.

Nasturtium is very effective for students, for those whose career requires intense intellectual activity, or for any stage of life where the intellect predominates.
If these head forces are allowed to prevail, the life of the individual becomes cold and disconnected from his physical body and the higher physical body of the Earth.
This imbalance predisposes the individual to many forms of physical illness, from colds and congestions in the head, to immune dysfunction and a general stiffening of the body.
The essence of the Nasturtium flower teaches the ego that the polarity of Light or consciousness must always be balanced with the opposite pole of Life or experience.

- Nasturtium gives strength and vitality to thought and also helps the individual direct their light into the practical experiences of everyday life and physical reality.

Nicotian

For those who use smoke to release their tensions, to master feelings and emotions.

For those who repress feelings and tend to hide behind hard identities. In the struggle to achieve balance, the individual needs to receive strength and stability from the Earth.

However, if the heart is not fully engaged in this process, etheric sensitivity and the higher feelings can be impeded.

This imbalance can be cured by Nicotiana or Flowering Tobacco.

The addiction to the nicotine contained in cigarettes, so widespread throughout the world, is a phenomenon born when Europeans discovered America and expanded rapidly.

In that same period, the individual's relationship with the Earth changed drastically.

Those who are addicted to nicotine look for a way to stay in touch with the earth and to bear the negative energies they feel around them; smoking is considered relaxing and pleasurable, although it causes a repression of feelings.

This reduction in sentimental life, accompanied by strong cardiac stimulation, gives the individual the possibility to adapt to the harshness and tension of the modern technological world and even to live in it without apparent problems.

- Nicotine flower essence is indicated in the treatment of tobacco addiction but is effective for a wide range of situations, as it represents a human condition that pervades the whole of modern civilization.

Nicotiana is a very important remedy for the heart, as it provides it with support in finding true energy, which is not separated from the life of feelings.

Oregon Grape

For those who have aggressive attitudes because they think the world is hostile to them; the person feels persecuted is always on the defensive and others isolate him for his attitudes.
This leads him into a state of solitude.

- Oregon Grape is indicated for people full of paranoia; they see hostility and disloyalty in the world and in the people around them.

These patterns were learned in childhood from family or upbringing and have not been remedied; on the contrary, they rot in the soul and continue to infect all human relationships and social situations.
Unfortunately, the individual oppressed by this state of paranoia creates the very reality that he projects, since those who are treated in a hostile or distrustful manner generally react by adopting the same attitude.

- Oregon Grape has many uses, but is best suited for the tension and malice that predominate in many city environments.

With Oregon Grape the individual learns to break the patterns of distrust he has behind him.
Instead, he realizes that he can pick up on the positive intentions of others and create situations that engender goodness and loving understanding.

Penstemon

Penstemon's lesson is reminiscent of the Biblical story of Job, in which life's harsh circumstances test one's deep faith and tenacity.

It seems that life has been unfair, one has lived through very shocking and painful experiences from which he cannot recover, because his evolutionary meaning is not understood.

- They are people who have good reasons to feel like victims; however, in these moments of pain and suffering, the individual must have the courage to rebuild himself and his faith to believe in a higher power.
- The essence allows the individual to call upon his own reserves of courage and resilience, which are normally inaccessible to human consciousness.

People who have suffered personal misfortunes and doubt whether they can continue facing life, the essence gives the feeling that it is possible to continue. In the face of discouragement, pessimism, self-pity, this essence gives resistance and strength to cope in the face of personal difficulties. Gives inner strength and stamina and perseverance to overcome obstacles.

It allows to do in the face of a defeat in sports competitions, exams. Recommended in old age to not give up and fight to live in the best possible way.

- It comes in handy when you feel life has been unfair.

The remedy brings courage, confidence to hold on in the difficult moments in which life puts us to the test. Useful in situations of extreme pain and physical suffering in terminal illnesses. It gives courage to accept and resist the process of agony and death.

Penstemon has tremendous empowering powers, allowing the individual to call upon their reserves of courage and resilience, which are normally inaccessible to human consciousness.

Peppermint

It is a tonic for those who feel tired and foggy, mentally numb.
Useful in apathy and post-prandial headaches.
The flower gives mental alertness and attention.

- Those in need of this remedy experience a strong conflict between the upper and lower part of their being, especially between the metabolic/digestive energies and the thought/creative energies.

In these cases, the metabolic energies overwhelm rationality with an excess of heat, making the mental capacity numb and sluggish.

- Peppermint has a cooling and warming effect at the same time.

It cools the lower organs, particularly the liver, so that the awareness can be freed to express itself in a higher way.
Peppermint also stimulates mental energies which, thus, have a "digestive property" of a superior nature, and make thought more lively, vital and penetrating.
Many people who need peppermint have major problems with nutrition and mindfulness.
They feel strongly the urge of food, only to find themselves sluggish and mentally incapacitated.
It's like two parts of the IT are fighting for attention.

- Peppermint gives great healing and balancing energy, freeing the mind to express higher thoughts and helping the vital energies of digestion to act in their rightful sphere.

Pink Monkeyflower

Essence for the fear of being exposed, the fear that others will see our suffering and our vulnerability; they are people who are afraid to express their true feelings, who cover up or are afraid to expose themselves, because they think that others cannot understand them.
They have difficulty opening up because they fear rejection and this leads them to hide essential parts of the self.
They avoid intimacy, because it could be the perfect ground for getting caught so they feel less vulnerable. They fear to bond deeply emotionally even if they long to be loved, but feel insecure, judged, or are afraid that some painful hidden secret may be discovered that causes them guilt or devaluation.

- Due to the concern to hide the past and their own suffering, these people prove to be closed, excessively shy or childish, sometimes false, and feel very inhibited in physical contact with others.

All this precludes them the possibility of satisfying the intense desire to be accepted by others and to establish deep emotional relationships. This can lead to an inability to bond deeply, fear of judgement, criticism, insecure, dependent, with sexual problems.

- Useful essence for the fragility of the heart (the person must learn that only by remaining open and putting one's own fragility at risk is it possible to experience the warmth of love and affection).
- The essence teaches the courage to take the risk of touching and being touched by others both emotionally and physically.

It helps to take emotional risks again, so they feel the love and touch they crave and desperately need.
Pink Monkeyflower gently opens up these people, helping them to take emotional risks again.
In this way, they begin to feel the love and touch they crave and

desperately need.

- In particular, Pink Monkeyflower is a remedy for the heart, as it teaches that only by remaining open and risking one's own fragility is it possible to experience the warmth of love and affection.

Pink Yarrow

Pliny tells us that the name of the genus was established by Linnaeus and derives from the belief that Achilles had used these plants during the siege of Troy to heal the wounds of his soldiers having learned from Chiron their medicinal virtues.
It protects people who are invaded by emotions because they are hypersensitive, so they get too involved in other people's problems and therefore don't know how to put a distance between themselves and others.

- The flower teaches to be compassionate without merging with the other.

They are hypersensitive people who cannot distinguish between genuine compassion and excessive identification with others, with their suffering and problems, thus becoming excessively vulnerable to their surroundings.

- It is therefore useful for therapists and for those who work in contact with suffering, but also for those who make the suffering of family and friends their own, reducing themselves to states of psychophysical exhaustion.

This flower protects the energy field of overly receptive people, gives greater objectivity and containment to learn to give a love that does not absorb, but spreads; who heals by adopting a compassionate but not fusional attitude. For those people who internalize other people's problems as their own.
They are very vulnerable, incorporate emotional qualities of others and have a tendency to feel awkward in a crowd; this hypersensitivity leads them to live exhausted by the emotional intensity.
It is therefore useful for weak and impressionable personalities, during pregnancy and adolescence.
In children it helps to protect them when there are family situations of trauma and drama. Very useful for twin brothers.

- Pink Yarrow flower essence gives greater objectivity and containment, teaching that true compassion comes from the heart, which is in contact with one's spiritual strength.

Thus, the person learns to give a love that does not absorb but spreads, which heals by adopting a compassionate but not fusional attitude.

Poison Oak

For people who are afraid to establish deep relationships because they think they might be hurt by the other person, for this reason they push intimacy away by emanating hostile attitudes.

Those who need Poison Oak actually have a very deep sensitivity within themselves and feel completely insecure about their personal boundaries.

They fear that if they are too open or too confidential, their personal defenses will be breached.

These people, therefore, rarely show their vulnerability and sensitivity, as they learn to deal with it by displaying an excessively harsh Martian exterior.

They erect negative barriers between themselves and others, showing hostility, anger, and irritability and thus maintaining an "emotional safe distance".

On a deeper level these people are afraid of their inner femininity or of being ensnared by feminine values.

This attitude can sometimes extend to feelings for Nature, so that the individual develops a relationship with Nature only through sport or with activities aimed at dominating the elements.

- Poison Oak teaches these individuals to gently open up by learning to recognize the sweetest aspect of themselves and to appropriate it.

In doing so, the individual creates boundaries that include rather than exclude, learning that the essential strength of the ego includes even the most sensitive and gentle aspects.

Pomegranate

For women who cannot choose between the role of mother and career woman and often feel frustrated in both roles. They are unable to express their creativity in a work occupation outside the family.

- It is a useful flower for sexual problems due to stress, fear of pregnancy, or other inner conflicts.
- For a positive and balanced female creativity, given that they are women who live a predominantly intellectual or artistic creativity to the detriment of the physical one.

It is useful in problems such as premenstrual syndrome and psychogenic infertility. It is also useful for men who have difficulty living the feminine (emotional, passive) part of their personality or integrating it with the masculine (rational, active) part. It is a flower that supports during pregnancy, facilitates childbirth, promotes fertilization and sexual satisfaction. In adolescence for a balanced development of reproductive energies and for a healthy attitude towards the first menstruation. It is an essence that integrates the soul and the animus, the Yin and the Yang. Balances female creativity, enhances intuition. It helps to accept one's femininity for women, while in men, it develops the maternal aspect.

- Pomegranate fosters a conscious alignment with the creative feminine self, so a woman can see her own destiny or choices more clearly.

Pomegranate helps the individual stay in touch with the Mother-Spirit of Love in all that she offers to the world.

Pretty Face

They are personalities who are overly concerned with their external appearance and who spend a lot of time and effort in being aesthetically better. They are seekers of physical perfection and are afraid of not being liked aesthetically and therefore being rejected. They are socially insecure and devalue themselves, feel inadequate and awkward, disheartened and pessimistic.

- The flower helps self-acceptance through contact with one's inner beauty. The beauty of the human being is spiritual, those who identify themselves or attribute excessive importance to their external appearance are easily conditioned by the aesthetic canons that society proposes.

And if he doesn't find himself in those canons, he can feel insecure, inadequate, feel rejection, ashamed. For those who, despite having normal traits, feel the need to change their appearance or for those who are afraid of getting old. Pretty Face changes the consciousness of the soul so that instead of looking outside, one finds the beauty inside. This essence is indicated for adolescents, obese people, people with physical handicaps, those who have a physical deformation because they were born there, or have had an accident and for pregnant women. Gives self-esteem and self-acceptance. For those with food problems, they see themselves as horrible, create an image of extreme fatness or thinness due to an inability to find the true source of beauty.

- In all these cases Pretty Face ensures that the individual no longer seeks beauty outside himself, but finds it within himself.

Pretty Face encourages the individual to be in touch with their true inner light and radiance, as they are the true components of beauty.

Purple Monkeyflower

For those who are afraid of the occult or are too superstitious.
It is the special flower for fears related to experiences of a spiritual or psychic nature.

- Like the other Mimulus (Monkeyflower) species, Purple Monkeyflower addresses the fear felt by the individual. Purple Monkeyflower is specifically indicated for fear related to experiences of a spiritual or psychic nature. More particularly, Purple Monkeyflower is of great benefit to individuals, whose great need for safety and salvation leads them to rely on conventional socio-religious structures, even if this often does not fulfill the real need for their soul evolution.

This creates an internal conflict between spiritual impulses and external conventions or expectations.
The fear of "going astray" and following one's own path can then be accentuated by harsh and rigid religious dogmas that include threats of punishment and condemnation.
Purple Monkeyflower is a powerful purifier and has the ability to debunk ideas based on cultural-religious superstition. Purple Monkeyflower is also indicated for intense fear, hallucinations or paranoia brought on by a sudden or unexpected spiritual initiation, such as in the case of drug use, ritual abuse or psychic manipulation.
In such cases the individual develops a deep fear of the spirit world, seeing it as demonic or terrifying.
The path to healing is that of courage to live one's true experience by facing spiritual phenomena in a calm and conscious way.
With this courage the individual is able to find true spiritual guidance, support and support for life on Earth.

Quaking Grass

For those who have problems interacting with the group (at work, at home, in sport) because they are too individualistic or get lost in the group. It helps to develop group awareness and creates balance between one's identity and that of others.

- It represents flexibility and the ability to relate to others while maintaining one's originality.

It promotes self-awareness and one's social role, mental flexibility and adaptability in the individual.

People unable to put their personal interests aside in favor of the group. It is difficult for them to work cooperatively with others and to accept points of view different from their own.

Intolerant, manipulative and rigid personalities.

They do not tolerate the opinions of others.

They neither receive nor contribute anything within a group, be it social, family, work or study.

It is an essence that grants flexibility and facilitates participation in the group; it makes the person more elastic and allows him to act according to a common purpose but without giving up his individuality.

Quaking Grass helps create a group awareness that is greater than any single person, yet takes into account each individual identity.

- Most importantly, Quaking Grass helps the individual see themselves within a greater social matrix.

Just as all parts of the physical body form a whole, so each individual can learn to conceive of his or her role within a larger social organism.

Such harmonious social consciousness is the special gift of the Quaking Grass flower.

Queen Anne's Lace

Lack of inner sight, that is, of psychic perception of oneself and of the world. Lack of intuition and inner sensitivity, inability to go beyond appearances.

- It teaches to go beyond appearances and to look at things with a more objective eye.
- This flower helps remove debris from emotional perspective that distorts "clear vision."
- It re harmonises the upper and lower chakras in order to stay connected to the Earth, maintaining a clear and objective vision and intuition.

They are personalities who avoid seeing what they don't want, what is painful and uncomfortable for them, or what could jeopardize the story of their life.

They generally have linear, rigid and structured thinking, with little openness to new knowledge. They read the circumstances and interpret them, but not in a very fortunate way.

They are not very objective, bad judges, without much criterion of reality and with a lack of common sense.

- Queen Anne's Lace is an important remedy for this transition of consciousness. It helps remove the debris from the emotional perspective that distorts a "clear view."

Such imbalances in the "third eye" chakra often arise from problems in the lower chakras, when emotional and instinctual energies such as sexuality are not well integrated by the individual.

Queen Anne's Lace brings both "higher" and "lower" energies into harmony, so that one stays in touch with the Earth, yet maintains a clear and objective vision and intuition.

Queen Anne's Lace is useful for many people who seek balanced psychic openness, or who have vision problems related to an emerging clairvoyance.

Quince

For those people with difficulty accepting their feminine aspects, hard and unable to open up to the ability to love and receptivity.

- For those who experience love and strength as antagonistic polarities.
- For women who deny their femininity as a way of demonstrating that they are strong.

Hardness and rigidity of character in emotional relationships; difficulty integrating masculine and feminine energies harmoniously within oneself; inability to express sweetness, tenderness, emotional warmth because the strong-willed and rational aspect of their personality represses these feelings (the mind repressing the heart). "Career" women who are unable to manage power harmoniously, who are unable to express their feminine qualities because they are too busy at work.

- The need to find a "feminine way" in managing power.

It can also be of great help to separated parents who have custody of their children, with whom they must in a certain sense simultaneously cover the maternal and paternal role or for all parents who must show their children both the sweet and protective aspect than firm discipline and objectivity. It restores, in women, their maternal capacity and confidence in feminine power.

- With Quince essence, the individual learns that true power is love and that true love also confers authority.

Rabbitbrush

It helps to have a clear view of multiple things happening simultaneously, without getting lost in details.
Gives the mind an alert and flexible state.
- Rabbitbbrush is one of the essences that stimulates and revitalizes the faculties of awareness.

Its particular property consists in the ability to combine two opposite poles: the focus and attention to detail with the global perspective capable of embracing the "big picture".
Most individuals are able to delve into only one of these two modes of awareness at best.
If they develop focus and concentration, it is only by cutting everything that might distract them out of their field of vision. If they learn to see the whole landscape of a situation, details are blurred, leaving only the broadest outlines visible.
The lesson for the person in need of Rabbitbrush is to maintain a clear and precise awareness of a range of single details, and at the same time to extend the field of awareness to include the broader principles of organization which relate the individual parts. .
The Rabbitbrush essence is indicated for people who feel overwhelmed by the large amount of details, or by the jumble of simultaneous happenings that require attention to each of them at the same time.
By developing the ability to integrate many details simultaneously and yet maintaining an awareness of the overall situation, the individual acquires great agility and flexibility.
- The person who unconsciously draws soul energy out of the body, fully engaging and focusing on the physical world, is unable to develop this potential and shrinks from the seemingly overwhelming challenges of modern life.

Red Clover

Hypersensitivity to emotions induced by the environment, gives calm and stability in emergency situations.
It is the expression of the ability to maintain conscious presence even in difficult situations.
The individual loses their identity and is used as a means to serve the needs of a negative force.
Helps maintain calm and awareness in the face of emotional excesses from the environment.
For those who are easily influenced by collective emotional states and easily get involved in fear, panic and mass hysteria. They get very distressed in chaotic situations, even if it doesn't hit them very closely.

- Great benefit if used by a group of people in situations of emergency, confusion and collective panic where it allows you to go back to being yourself and think calmly and mentally clearly.

It restores harmony in some unpleasant circumstances that can occur within a family, for example when the misunderstanding and the quarrel between two members extends, also involving the others or when one of them is in danger of life and the entire household panics.

- This essence is recommended for those people who always see a negative future in the place and situation in which they are living.

In vaporizer, when there is agitation in the environment.
Red Clover Flower Essence is a powerful purifier and balancer; it is particularly related to the psychic properties of blood, in which each individual's spiritual ego resides.

Rosemary

For people who are pale, low blood pressure, introverted, physically ethereal with cold hands and feet. They live a lot in the head and therefore have no roots in the earth, or they have suffered violence and reject their bodies.

- Rosemary flower essence is a strong remedy that causes awakening and incarnation, it is indicated for those individuals whose incarnation is weak or problematic, especially when the higher spiritual or thought faculties fail to act adequately through the physical vehicle.

This results in a state of reduced Consciousness in the body, with a tendency towards mindlessness or forgetfulness or hypoglycemia. In particular, the individual's energies lack warmth and fully embodied presence.
Literally, this means that the physical extremities of the body are often cold and lifeless.
On deeper levels, this lack of warmth has to do with a sense of insecurity in one's physical body.
This can sometimes be attributed to a karmic disposition of the individual, who feels ambivalent about his or her incarnation and has learned to use spiritual forces outside of the material world. Very often this disease of the soul is caused by a trauma suffered in early childhood, in which physical abuse and the stress of the environment have forced the individual to leave his body, so that he no longer believes in his connection with the physical world.
Rosemary gives these people the ability to feel comfortable and confident in their physical body.
With these renewed forces, the flame of the spirit burns more brilliantly in the body and gives its light and consciousness to the physical world.

Sage

To learn and reflect on life experiences, especially the ability to feel inner peace and wisdom.

- It can be helpful during various transitional stages, where one needs to go back and consider unfolding life events.

Useful in the advanced stage of life, as it helps to understand what has been experienced, to recognize life's purposes, to heal and to advise others.

- It gives inner peace and wisdom.
- It helps to remember life experiences and gives the ability to reflect and understand until you have a feeling of inner fullness.

Individuals who have difficulty learning from life experiences and repeat mistakes, repeat cycles of behaviors and experiences and thinking that this is their destiny. Little able to discriminate, with difficulty at introspection, they must discover the inner wisdom.

Narcissistic personalities with learning disabilities and stubborn. Essence indicated in situations where the person feels the need for the advice of more mature (wise and experienced) people to feel contained and be able to make the appropriate decisions.

- With Sage, the individual comes more in touch with their own higher spirituality. By recognizing the spiritual meaning and purpose of life, the individual gains profound wisdom to heal and counsel others.

Sagebrush

The druids considered it a sacred plant and used it to weave the garlands to wear on the head during the summer solstice rite.
For those who tend to emphasize the illusory aspects of being, identifying with what they possess and with their social role and thus precluding the possibility of spiritual evolution.
It favors the discernment between the essential and the superfluous.
For those who must free themselves from ancient habits and lifestyles and get rid of old schemes, false securities and past identities that are no longer suitable for life circumstances.

- It helps to free oneself from things of the past, whether they are accumulated material objects, rather than family addictions, useful for preparing for the future.

Often, the Higher Self intervenes by establishing a condition for purging the false personality through disease or misfortune.
Sagebrush helps the individual to get in touch with his most naked and essential self, since it is there that true freedom and great spiritual forces reign.
When the individual recognizes what is absolutely essential for his identity and abandons what no longer serves his evolution, he takes a step forward in his destiny with a much greater force of discrimination and inner freedom.

Saguaros

It allows the understanding of one's origins and one's past.
This usually occurs in adolescence and early adulthood and depends on the fact that the individual is not aware that they are solely responsible for their own life.
People who find themselves in conflict with authority and power figures especially with the father and male figures.
They don't accept being told what to do, they don't let themselves be guided, they feel forced and they react by opposing it. They have difficulty taking on the role of parent or authority.
- The flower gives the sense of tradition, of descent and gives the ability to learn from the elderly.
- Ideal for conflicts associated with the image of the father.
- It allows you to abide by the laws by respecting authority and traditions instead of competing or fighting unnecessarily.

The essence addresses the rebellious tendencies of the emotional life, refining them and making them positive qualities of awareness and introspection. Saguaro can also be helpful when the individual needs a deeper understanding of their traditions, ancestry or culture, or needs to establish a more conscious relationship with the authority and guidance of older people.
By actively embracing and understanding one's past, the individual is free to grow and change in a more conscious and clear way.

Saint John's Wort

It is the flower linked to darkness and sleep such as children's incontinence, night sweats, nightmares, sleepwalking.

- Extremely sensitive, they capture the anxieties of the outside world. They are people who burn easily in sunlight or have rashes, burn easily, suffer from strong heat or light damages them.

They may be afraid of fire or bothered by bright lights.
Nightmares, childhood fears, phobias, sleepwalking, night terrors, dreamy states, distorted states of consciousness, people with low vitality, very nervous. Accident ideas.
People who can't stand clothes that are too tight. Useful during menopause or premenstrual syndrome.
For those who live in a dreamy state of consciousness, with a deficit in the internal perception of their body schema.
For those suffering from known and unknown fears, real or dreamed. Vulnerable to negative experiences and influences during sleep. Tendency to out-of-body experiences.

- The flower offers protection and guidance in distorted states. Frees the individual of fears and strengthens him. Eliminate nightmares.

It gives the ability to experience and trust the inner light as a source of consciousness ("The lamp of Diogenes").
On a deeper level of transformation, Saint John's Wort assists the individual in spreading light throughout the body and the Earth.
Instead of experiencing light as an external and merely physical reality, it can act within the ego as a spiritual force that illuminates and anchors the consciousness.

Scarlet Monkeyflower

For people who try to control themselves in everything they do as they fear their own feelings and repress them especially the strong and "red" ones such as anger, hatred, jealousy and aggression, because they are afraid of losing control or fear the judgment of others.

- They fear their "shadow side" or lower emotions.

But they get to a point where they can't take it anymore and break out with angry reactions. These outbursts confirm fear and the need for control and a vicious circle is created from which one is no longer able to get out.

Scarlet Monkeyflower empowers the courage to fully acknowledge and confront those feelings so they can be integrated rather than repressed.

It dispels fear, gives inner honesty and clarity, promotes acceptance and understanding of strong emotions and stimulates the individual to harmoniously manifest self-expression and affirmation.

The lesson to be learned is to face our dark parts and control our internal violence, overcome blocks and resolve situations of power and anger in interpersonal relationships.

- Scarlet Monkeyflower gives courage to fully acknowledge and face such feelings.

Scarlet Monkeyflower imparts emotional depth, honesty and vitality to the individual on their journey to true wholeness.

Scotch Broom

It belongs to the Leguminosae family and owes its popular name to its hard stems which were used as brooms. This and the narcotic properties that are attributed to this plant may have been the reason for the ancient association between witches and brooms. This is also why it was used against spells.

For those who are oppressed by despair and pessimism not only with regard to themselves, but also with everything that happens around them. The depression experienced by such people is characterized not only by feelings about their own lives, but also about the world as a whole and about their relationship to world events. For people with little tenacity, little perseverance. He has a sense of depression and heaviness about both his own life and the future of the world.

Feelings of being useless and that one's life is useless.

They are generally sad people, very anxious, disheartened, who always interpret every circumstance in a destructive and apocalyptic way.

Scotch Broom gives tenacity and strength, allowing the individual to move from their personal desperation to being of service and caring for the welfare of the world.

- Scotch Broom helps the individual meet the challenges of our times as an opportunity for personal growth and to help others. In making this transition, the individual moves from his unconscious identification with the darkness of the world, to a more hopeful and positive vision of the world's future.

Self Heal

It helps to stimulate the body's ability to heal itself (for example, in long-term illnesses or with unsuccessful treatments). They are people who are very dependent on external help and therefore lack a spiritual motivation for healing or who have become discouraged because they have tried many therapies without success.
They have lost faith in their own ability to be well and have delegated this inner responsibility to therapists or others.

- This flower stimulates understanding and acceptance of suffering, gives confidence in one's abilities, allowing the individual to take direct responsibility for their own well-being and to find the inner strength necessary to start the healing process.

For those people who have to wake up their internal healers because they have little self-confidence and acceptance and who try, treatment after treatment, the cure, without achieving success.
The core of one's personality is found awash with a negative anchoring to the inner forces of the individual, no therapy can bring about true healing unless the individual is stimulated and motivated within to seek and affirm the wholeness of life.
The flower develops the internal healing power. It allows you to find internal reasons to feel good. It gives trust and acceptance.

- It is a very beneficial remedy for those who encounter great obstacles in their recovery from a physical, mental and spiritual point of view.

The great lesson and the powerful gift of Self Heal is to give the ego the possibility to believe and to affirm its recovery and healing abilities, being in contact with its intrinsic beneficial resources of life and healing potential.

Shasta Daisy

For those who intellectualize reality too much, considering information as fragments rather than as parts of a whole.
They are people who get lost in details and are too analytical and in doing so lose their understanding of the larger meanings and patterns of mental and emotional experience.
- This flower maintains the vision of the global, the possibility of synthesizing ideas into a whole.

Remedy recommended for intellectuals, researchers, scholars, teachers and for all dispersed and confused people who find it difficult to achieve a holistic vision of the reality in which they have been inserted.
This flower favors the evolutionary process, both because it facilitates intuitive understanding and develops the ability to harmoniously synthesize heterogeneous information, and because it spiritualises the intellect, allowing the person to acquire a clear awareness of the totality in which he is inserted.
Shasta Daisy imparts insight into the broader meanings and patterns of mental and emotional experience.
- Shasta Daisy assists the individual in gaining an archetypal or all encompassing consciousness, stimulating the great energies of intelligence and insight into life experience.

Shooting Star

For people who feel alienated from everything, different, out of place. They have the feeling of alienation: of not being part of the family, of the planet, or they feel trapped in a body that they don't feel.
It helps in difficult pregnancies and supports premature babies.
- On a deeper level, Shooting Star teaches such individuals that Earth is the right place to humanize one's cosmic consciousness, as it is the place to learn love that comes from the heart.

Snapdragon

For those with great verbal aggression.
He is hostile, sarcastic, impetuous, his jaws are always tense, the constant need to chew; they are people with a strong physical presence, energetic and endowed with a great badly channeled will.
In some cases, these energies are so pronounced that they dominate the other chakras.
In other cases, these forces may have been repressed by culture, resulting in an inappropriate release of energy in the body.
With these two types of imbalance, the individual misdirects the digestive and sexual energies, which in fact belong to the lower energy centers, by misdirecting them through the communication centres.
The word is misused, harshly and destructively, with a tendency toward biting sarcasm or scathing criticism.
There may be a strong tension in the jaws and mouth, a grinding of the teeth or the need to eat food, which stimulates a constant biting and chewing.
Snapdragon helps these people get their powerful metabolic and sexual energy back in the right direction by directing it into the right channels.

- On a deeper level, Snapdragon helps the individual distinguish the use of creative energies, especially those that radiate from the lower energy centers and those that are used for speech.

By making the relationship between these energy centers harmonious, the individual evolves in the use of his own creative power.

Star Thistle

Indicated for the "fear of lack", or for those who think that there is no abundance. When the personality is not in touch with the spiritual light, it can feel a sense of emptiness, instability and uncertainty which is often compensated for by excessive preoccupation with material things.
This makes us grumpy, distrustful and stingy, because we try to accumulate as much as possible and keep what we have, deluding ourselves that we can fill our inner emptiness in this way.

- They are afraid of losses, so they accumulate, and this gives them security for the future.

They are possessive, stingy people, they lack generosity, they always need external security.
They aim more at material things than at emotional ones. They have no faith in a superior providence.
However, accumulating wealth does not make them happy, on the contrary they always feel very alone and withered. There can often be a problem with bonding with the mother. It also promotes generosity and develops awareness that by sharing one's resources the individual is not impoverished, but internally enriched.
Often withdrawn and adverse to society, they do not have the opportunity to learn to trust, or to share their ego or resources in an open and generous way.
Regardless of possible wealth or social status, these people are often deeply lonely, feeling completely parched and unfulfilled.

- Star Thistle helps to be more self-confident and therefore to be less dependent on external things. Through giving that the individual finds inner nourishment, and it is with the participation of the ego that the individual enriches and fills himself abundantly.

Star Tulips

To help us listen to our inner guidance.
Helps remember dreams, meditate and pray.
- It helps women who are too harsh and men who deny their feminine side.
- It can be termed a "hearing remedy" as it helps the individual to become more aware of subtler influences or guidance from the higher realms.

This remedy is very beneficial for those who cannot be in touch with their Higher Self or cannot meditate or fold efficiently.
Star Tulip has a strong relationship with the "soul" or inner feminine, it is an excellent remedy for men who have denied their softer and more receptive aspect or for women who have created a defensive shield.
Star Tulip opens and sensitizes the soul, making it more aware of its links with the higher worlds.
It favors dreaming, prayer, meditation and all intuitive abilities.
It is an important essence for the initial stages of the therapeutic process, as it helps to open and "soften" the emotional life, allowing the individual to recognize and retrieve important information regarding the inner healing process.
- In its maximum expression, Star Tulip builds a goblet-shaped vase in the human soul, in order to create the ability to receive and contain the highest thought and inspiration.

Sticky Monkeyflower

For those who are afraid of intimacy and sexuality understood as deep contact with each other. Often these people can mask their fear by seeking lots of sexual intercourse that does not involve true heartfelt sympathy, or on the contrary they avoid any kind of sexual contact. This flower helps integrate the physical and spiritual aspects of love. People dominated by the fear of demonstrating their true feelings and being discovered by others in their affections.

- For those who repress themselves, they self-censor; those who would like to express their feelings of love and are unable to do so and therefore fall into loneliness. On many occasions, their blocks are due to unprocessed sorrows in previous relationships.
- The flower gives warmth in the intimate relationship, security, expressiveness, adjustment, clarity, acceptance, joy and depth in the affections. The lesson that makes learning is to have the courage to show true feelings, learn to understand the meaning of sexual activity.

It can be of great help in adolescence to overcome embarrassment and shyness related to sexual feelings and desires. Through sexuality one can enter into deep contact with another human being and thus experience the strongest ecstasy and the greatest pain of the soul. So the fear in these people is to expose their ego to another human being of being vulnerable or rejected. This is why sexuality is superficial and devoid of real participation.

In menopause it is useful for developing new models of intimacy, transforming sexual identity by making it part of the passage of menopause.

Sunflower

These flowers have the characteristic that they become heavier as they grow, and if they do too much, the stem can no longer support them and fall. Its height can reach 4 meters, they are oriented towards the sun on which their development depends. The sunflower is the representation of the Sun which, with its harmonious and balanced expression of male creative energy, illuminates the individual and heals with its warmth.

- Particularly suitable for all people who have problems emanating this solar power in a balanced way, therefore they have an unbalanced sense of ego, that is, in excess or in defect: for those who are too arrogant and presumptuous, they are vain narcissists (the brilliance of the sun it shines too brightly and dazzles, you need to bring the heat out), or for those who underestimate themselves or suffer from an inferiority complex, are insecure and always feel inadequate (the brightness of the ego is obscured, you need to give light to the soul).

The person absorbs the lunar qualities of receptivity and nourishment from the mother, while from the father he learns the solar qualities of the shining, expressive ego. This essence cures problems or distortions in the individual's relationship with the masculine, often associated with a conflicted or defective relationship with the father in childhood and is equally important for both men and women. Useful in adolescent problems when there is a conflict with authority and with the father figure.

Improve parents' relationships with their sons.

When the Sunflower individual learns how to tap into this great solar force within themselves, they are truly able to give a precious gift to other humans and to the Earth by caring for and healing.

Sweet Peas

For people who can't find roots anywhere and can't integrate anywhere.
Useful for those who have undergone many transfers in their life, or for children who are adopted.
Many individuals live as pilgrims, desperately seeking their place on earth. When this condition is too accentuated, the individual gets lost in wandering being unable to create true bonds of involvement and commitment with society.
Such people move from place to place, or from group of friends to group of friends, without ever really becoming involved.
They consolidate their position as "outsiders" and are deprived of true growth of soul, as they are unable to put down their roots in family or social life.
At the heart of the suffering of those in need of Sweet Pea is a deep sense of precariousness.

- Sweet Pea people do not have within them "a sense of place," or love of the Earth.

This alienation can derive from the experience of real wandering or continuous forced displacement lived in childhood.
This imbalance is also related to urban and suburban living conditions, whether large housing developments, city slums, or squalid suburban developments, which deprive the individual of his or her natural involvement and connection with the Earth and the forces of Nature.
Sweet Pea helps these people get in touch with their feelings about "their own home".
By becoming aware of this suffering that has darkened the ego, the individual can begin to heal and find his true bond with the Earth and with other human beings.

Tansy

For those who are lethargic, apathetic, lazy, who tend to escape from reality by sleeping. They procrastinate and are unable to act immediately or directly, as if they were indifferent or careless.
In fact, this has become a way of maintaining emotional detachment in situations. The flower helps to be decisive, direct in reactions, aware of the path to follow.

- The essence of the Tansy flower heals the ego consciousness in a very special way. Those in need of this remedy have a great deal of sluggish, lethargic energy; very often he is indecisive, tends to procrastinate decisions or commitments, and appears lazy, indifferent or careless.

While their willpower is effectively blocked, it is generally not effective to heal this person directly at the level of willpower or physical energy.
The insight into the healing method comes from understanding why these people hold back from expressing their ego. This type of person reacts to intense oppression, excitement, or any pressure or tension, by withdrawing and constricting physical energy. Sometimes this is just a temporary reaction to life circumstances, but generally you will understand that this way of managing energy is part of a deeply unconscious and deeply ingrained pattern associated with family and childhood traumas.

- Tansy people have been exposed to many chaotic, confusing situations, emotional instability or even violence and have learned to repress their gut reaction in order to be at peace or to avoid further emotional pressure. "They ingenuity", as a defense mechanism to maintain an emotional detachment and to support situations.

T

ansy stimulates self-awareness in these people, helping them get in touch with their own strength and purpose.

In this way, such individuals become more assertive and direct in their reaction to others and to life, and come to realize their true self more fully.

Tiger Lily

Helps to overcome egocentrism for people who find it difficult to work in groups because they are aggressive and competitive, have an authoritarian attitude.
There is an excessive spirit of competition and the desire to get or keep power.
Useful for women with too masculine characteristics or in hormonal imbalances of menopause in which the greater male energy enters the consciousness.

- It is a useful remedy for both men and women because it favors the expression of the feminine aspects of the personality, harmonizing them with the masculine ones.

The ability to interact positively with others and within society depends on the ability to develop understanding, acceptance and respect for others.

- This essence develops the sense of cooperation and understanding, favors the overcoming of the limited self-centered and personal vision and allows one to perceive a wider reality, towards values that include the whole and the totality.

Useful essence especially for those who consider themselves separate from others or fighting against others instead of working for the common good.
Work on the rivalry archetype.
It is an essence that can also be used to treat hostile or aggressive dogs or cats.

Trillium

For those who, rich or poor, have unbridled ambition and think that happiness can only be accessed through material goods. Thus he falls back into forms of greed and lust for power.

- Trillium flower essence is a very effective cleanser and balancer for the lowest energy center, termed the survival (base) chakra.
- The person in need of Trilliurn has a disproportionate amount of energy directed towards attaining personal power and wealth.

This excessive concern for personal welfare dominates over all other more altruistic feelings.

Such a person easily falls prey to the forces of materialism and greed, feeling the need for many possessions and other forms of material wealth and power.

Trillium may also be suitable for those who are poor but believe that the acquisition of wealth and power brings fulfillment.

- This imbalance of the soul can also be reflected in the body, especially when the body retains too much matter and does not eliminate enough toxins.

Since their awareness is limited to the physical plane, such individuals can measure their self-worth only with a material yardstick. Trillium encourages these individuals to shift their awareness to a level beyond the personal, to derive a sense of personal well-being from the relationship with the higher power. Once the forces held in the lower chakra are purified and released, such people will have a great ability to take possession of the spiritual forces and make them available to others and to the Earth.

Trumpet Vine

For those who have difficulty speaking in public and for those who speak in a very weak voice.
They are people who do not have the ability to speak clearly or have problems with verbal language, they make speeches that are too boring, concise or mechanical.
Trumpet Vine Flower Essence is indicated for speech that tends to be rote, dull or too terse and can be very helpful for various speech impediments such as stuttering.
It does not directly address fear or nervousness, but is still beneficial for many people who contain their expression due to fear or shyness.

- With the help of Trumpet Vine, the individual will be able to get in touch with the life energy that resides in the lower chakras and integrate their life force into verbal language; then bring one's awareness and interest to the expression itself, instead of focusing on how others may perceive or judge it.

Trumpet Vine awakens the warm and colorful life of the soul's feelings, helping these qualities to flow into verbal language.
As the individual learns to communicate and express himself, he develops his creative capacity to share his unique essence with others and with the world.

Violet

For those people who are so shy and reserved and sensitive that they can't stand the group, because they are afraid of being overwhelmed by it; so they isolate themselves, but they suffer a lot.
They love silence.

- Violet-type energies are very refined, full of exquisite but delicate sweetness.

These people desire deep contact with others, but generally hold back from doing so due to a sense of fragility in group situations and a fear that the sense of self will be lost or submerged.
This type of individual often chooses a lifestyle or occupation where they can work quietly and alone.
The Violet personality feels great warmth within, but appears cold and detached to others; also the body and especially the hands can be wet and cold.
Since such individuals can find very few people who are able to understand and accept their shyness, they suffer from loneliness, as they would like to give themselves more.
The key to their resolution lies in the ability to believe in the affection of others.

- Like the violet, whose essential fragrance cannot be perceived until the sun shines upon it and the air shakes it, so the Violet type must learn to let one's essence express itself through others.

The essence of the Violet flower helps these individuals to no longer fear losing their self, but to trust in revealing it to others, so that its wonderful nature can be shared with the world.

Yarrow

For people who, being very sensitive, are vulnerable because they feel and absorb the influences of the negative environment and others.
They tend to get tired and exhausted easily.
People typically in need of this remedy are easily affected by their surroundings and may be prone to many forms of environmental disease, allergies or various psycho-somatic illnesses.
Such people have an amazing ability to heal, counsel or teach, as they are quick to receive psychic impulses and understand the pain and suffering of others.
At the same time they tend to discharge easily and are quite vulnerable to negative thoughts or intentions from others.

- Yarrow literally "stitches up" the too porous aura of such individuals, so as not to make it "disperse" too much in the surrounding environment.

It also helps to balance and stabilize the abundant light that spreads in the higher energy centers, directing it to the lower centers, so that the ego gains greater vitality and solidity.
Yarrow flower essence is almost universally applicable and should be included in many blends indicated for the profound changes of the individual in our times.
Yarrow endows the ego with a shield of brilliant Light that protects the spiritual essence, allowing healing properties to flow freely from one individual to another.

Yarrow Special Formula

Yarrow, Arnica and Echinacea, GoldenYarrow and Pink Yarrow based on sea water combined with the fresh tinctures of these three plants

Initially the Yarrow special formula essence was created in the period of the Chernobyl nuclear disaster of 1986.

It protects against radiation, radiotherapy and cobalt therapy, electromagnetic waves, X-rays, and video terminals.

Subsequently, the last two flowers were added to make the protective spectrum that this composition has on all levels much more complete.

Its purpose is to strengthen and protect against toxic, geopathic, environmental influences, and other hazards of modern life and technology.

- Yarrow Special Formula is indicated not only for direct exposure to nuclear emissions, but also for the many ways in which nuclear radiation and other highly toxic and aberrant forms of energy poison the modern world.

These include video terminals, X-rays, radiotherapy, high-altitude radiation, airport control systems and electromagnetic fields.

Yarrow Special Formula is an immensely important remedy; it acts as a shield against the destructive forces that threaten and plague human life and the planet, putting into action powerful revitalizing and restorative properties.

Yarrow Special Formula is great, not just for air travel, but also in urban environments, such as when you're cycling, in subways and buses, or driving through traffic.

Yellow Star Tulip

For those who are insensitive to the sufferings of the world, of the Earth, have no awareness of the consequences of their actions towards others.
It raises awareness to develop listening to the other and empathy.

- Yellow Star Tulip refines the individual, developing his ability to be receptive and social in an intuitive way.

It acts on the ego not so much inwardly, but rather helps the individual to direct all that he has developed in his inner life outwards as a gift to help and heal others, or working with the forces of Nature.
Yellow Star Tulip develops the quality of empathy, so that one can intuit and act upon the deeper meaning and message of other beings.
Yellow Star Tulip, in particular, makes you sensitive to the suffering of others, as without empathy you cannot be truly compassionate.
It can sometimes act as a "karmic truth serum" so that one can feel the results of one's actions towards others more intensely.
Yellow Star Tulip breaks down negative and selfish barriers to ego, so that one can learn to make more sensitive contact with others and truly learn from others.
Yellow Star Tulip is especially important for people practicing therapists or teachers who need to broaden and refine their empathy skills.
It can also be used more broadly to heal relationships and to help people exhibiting extreme states such as sociopathological tendencies.

Yerba Santa

The flower comes from a Spanish term which means "holy herb" and is aimed at the health of the human soul within the heart which must remain open and free. But it is a sensitive and vulnerable part to the emotions of the soul.
If these emotions are not used actively, they are stored and buried in this part of the heart; thus, the flower is useful for despondency and deep sadness with tightness in the chest.
Internalized anguish and melancholy because the emotions have been repressed and make people appear wasted, as if they were wasting away.

- It is for all pain and anguish related to the "heart", to affections, repressed or excessively internalized anguish which is reflected in disturbances in the chest area. It concerns emotional shocks such as the loss of a loved one even in childhood, a divorce, traumas experienced in the family, all situations whose pain has been suffocated.

It gives the ability to let emotions flow freely, to expel deep pain and grief gently.
With this "blessed" flower, the person re-establishes his or her sanctuary, freeing the human heart to experience the world with a renewed emotionality, full of light and more spacious.

- For people who have feelings of oppression, who suffer from deep sadness and keep traumatic memories in their memory. "They suffer in silence." Patients with a propensity for psychosomatic illnesses who drown in their own "air."

The flower frees from oppressive experiences, calms down in case of unpleasant effects produced by other essences.
The lesson to learn is to learn to breathe with the "heart" and let the pain out.
Yerba Santa gradually recovers the temple of the heart, making it more spacious and filled with light.

- With Yerba Santa, blessed flower, the individual re-establishes his own sanctuary, making the human heart free to experience the world with a renewed emotionality.

Zinnia

For those who have forgotten the ability that children have to have fun.
They are too serious, gloomy people.
This flower makes you rediscover the pleasure of laughter and happiness.
Humor is a peculiarity of mankind.
Other forms of life certainly experience joy and pleasure, but humor means being able to get out of the ego and not take yourself so seriously, it is the human being, with his pronounced sense of the ego, who has developed the property of 'humor and badly needs it.
The ability to laugh at oneself or to be "light-hearted" is literally a necessary balance to the grim heaviness of self-consciousness.
Zinnia is a truly wonderful remedy for this state of mind. Zinnia helps the ego to get in touch with your inner child.
Every child is born with the innate ability to laugh and play, to enter life with the full exuberance of a winged soul.
The adult ego too often suffocates and suppresses this part of itself.

- Zinnia is clearly indicated for people who are too austere and serious, who take themselves and life too seriously or tend towards overwork or other extreme forms.

Zinnia's message is not that life has to be frivolous or irresponsible, but rather that qualities of playfulness and laughter can be transferred to work and daily life.

- The essence of the Zinnia flower imparts the quality of humor, teaching that the individual "enlivened by a sense of humor" truly follows a balanced spiritual path.